REJECTION

Identifying and Eliminating the Rejection Mindset

Greg Mitchell

Front and Back Cover Design: Steven Ciaccio

English Version Print Edition ISBN: 979-8-9907176-0-2

English Version Kindle Edition ISBN: 979-8-9907176-1-9

Library of Congress Cataloging-in-Publication Data has been applied for.

Printed in the United States of America

Table of Contents

Dedication

To my parents Wayman and Nelda Mitchell:
You broke the curse of rejection off your lives and raised us with love and acceptance. I am forever grateful. The reference points you set for us have blessed my life, my marriage, my family, and every place I minister – to this day.
You, being dead, still speak. Hebrews 11:4

To the congregations where we have had the privilege to Pastor - Launceston, Footscray, Dandenong, Eldorado Park and Prescott:
You allowed me to develop in ministry and become more effective as a Pastor. In each place, I learned lessons that have helped me to become the man and Pastor I am today. Your support, prayers, and patience each contributed something to my development along the way, so any good God accomplishes through Lisa and I – you have a part in it.

To the love of my life – my wife Lisa:
You put up with me, and prayed for me as I grew and worked out some of my own rejection issues. We have grown up together and grown together. There is no me without you. My life is rich with you in it. I love you!

Foreword

"You should write another book!" I said as I was having coffee with Greg Mitchell and several other pastors in Prescott, Arizona, after a recent Bible Conference.

I said these words considering the incredible success of his first book, "Healing Power," which inspired and helped multitudes of believers and leaders. It motivated and instructed them to experience for themselves success in ministering God's healing power.

"Uprooting Rejection" was first taught by Greg Mitchell as an Adult Bible Hour series, and these notes were made available to Pastors and Fellowship churches around the world for their congregations. I did just that. I taught the series in my church in Perth, West Australia, and the help people received by applying these principles was astounding! I constantly received testimonies of freedom and deliverance from people who had been plagued with this mindset for many years. To have these ideas, principles, and practical help in book form was, to me, an exciting thought.

My interest in this subject began at an early stage in my ministry. While attending a Bible Conference in 1988 in Perth, I received a word of prophecy from the founding pastor of our Fellowship, Wayman Mitchell. He spoke about how he had received this scripture early in his ministry and wanted to share it with me.

Isaiah 49:25 NKJV *But thus says the LORD: "Even the captives of the mighty shall be taken away, And the prey of the terrible be delivered; For I will contend with him who contends with you, And I will save your children.*

"This is a deliverance scripture," Pastor Mitchell said, "and you need to look into spiritual things to provide answers and freedom for others."

Not long after this, I read my first book about rejection. The book described rejection as the satanic masterstroke, the undiagnosed malady in the body of Christ. I decided I needed to know more if I was to effectively minister the gospel to this broken world. Thus began my journey to research and learn about this critical topic.

After teaching from the notes I received from Greg Mitchell and reading an early copy of this book, I am confident that the principles within its pages will be a very beneficial resource. Not only would this aid those wanting to overcome their own personal issues but also those who would like to minister healing and deliverance to others more successfully.

I have had the privilege of knowing Greg Mitchell for many decades and have seen the incredible faith, hard work, and wisdom he has in life and in ministering the Word of God. I highly recommend this book and the expertise of the author. Greg Mitchell has keen insight and skill. He has worked hard to bring this vital topic to life in this practical but deeply insightful book.

As you read these pages, I trust you will find God's freedom and experience renewed hope for a brighter future. May these life-changing principles impact not only your life but also the lives of those you are ministering to as we all endeavor to "Uproot Rejection."

Daryl Elliott | Perth, West Australia

Preface

"What is wrong with me?" the man asked me. He sat with his body tensed and his fists balled up. He looked frustrated and exhausted. *"Every new relationship I make, every new job I start, in just a short amount of time, I am offended by something that is said or something that happens. I react badly, which either ends the relationship or job or makes it awkward, and I have to move on. I spend half the time being hurt or upset and the other half worrying about what people think of me. I'm driving my family crazy and driving myself crazy. Why can't I just feel normal, like everybody else?"* Like many others I have counseled through the years, this man recognized how he felt and reacted was not helpful but had no idea why and certainly no idea of how to change.

People fascinate me. As a Pastor – I am in the people business. I have been called by God to minister for Him - to people. From my earliest ministry, as I tried to help people, I became puzzled by the decisions people made, the actions they took, and the reactions I saw to various situations and conversations. I saw people make choices, take actions, and react in often unhealthy ways. Many of these were totally unreasonable and usually destructive to their lives, relationships, and walk with God. Even in myself, I recognized that, at times, I acted or reacted in ways that were not helpful.

So I began to ask questions: WHY? Why do people choose, act, or react in unreasonable or unhealthy ways? What is the root of these things? How do people get this way? I asked these questions to gain understanding – so I could help people spiritually.

As a very young Pastor, I came across a book dealing with the issue of rejection. It didn't give many practical ways to deal with it the problem, but it opened my eyes to the issue of rejection. It answered many of the questions I was asking about people and questions they were asking me. From that time, I began to search God's word, pray for insight, ask questions, and read any book I could get my hands on to try and help people. I have preached many sermons on rejection through the years.

In 2021, I began teaching a series in the Adult Sunday School Class at the church I Pastor in Prescott, Arizona (The Potter's House). I originally intended for it to be a 4-6 week series, but from the opening lesson, it was clear that this was going to meet deep needs and help people in practical ways. So, I went deeper than I had in my previous ministry and expanded the series to 16 lessons.

"Uprooting Rejection" was the first series of mine that was shown in many churches throughout our Fellowship. That showed me that God was using it to meet needs in people. I began to get feedback and testimonies of how much people were helped, healed, and delivered by the teaching. Since then, many people have encouraged me to write a book based on the series.

So, here we go. This book will look at issues in people's pasts to help bring freedom. I stress that I am not a psychologist or simply advocating therapy to try and help. I believe in two foundational things:

    1.   I believe that God is the answer to every human problem. My aim is to turn your eyes to Jesus Christ, who is the true source of all freedom:
        a. **John 8:36 NCV** *36 So if the Son makes you free, you will be truly free.*
    2. I believe in supernatural deliverance and the power of truth to bring freedom
        a. **John 8:32 NKJV** *32 And you shall know the truth, and the truth shall make you free.*

I encourage anyone reading this (or listening to it) to take the time to note the scriptures I use in each lesson and read them, study them, and pray over them for yourself. Ask God to not just give you information – but <u>revelation</u>.

__Ephesians 1:17-18 NKJV__ [17]that the God of our Lord Jesus Christ, the Father of glory, may give to you the spirit of wisdom and revelation in the knowledge of Him, [18]the eyes of your understanding being enlightened; that you may know what is the hope of His calling, what are the riches of the glory of His inheritance in the saints.

If God gives you revelation, He can then bring healing and deliverance from rejection.

There will also be written testimonies, and links to video testimonies and actual prayers throughout the book that you can pray along with, and pray over yourself.

The QR codes will allow you to see the videos: Testimonies and prayers. Point a phone or tablet with a camera at the QR code. A yellow box will pop up that says "qrco.de" Click on it, and it will take you to the video.

If your device doesn't have connectivity (or you find this step difficult), you can go to the media link page directly and access all media for this book.

https://www.prescottpottershouse.com/uprooting-rejection-media

Pastor Greg Mitchell

Prescott, Arizona

May 2024

Chapter 1
Roots of Rejection

Pastor Rick Renner tells of a time when he was sick for a long time in Junior High School, so he missed some basic math principles he needed for Algebra class. Consequently, he was behind the rest of the class. His teacher mocked him for not knowing basic things and started calling him 'Stupid.' She would call the attendance roll: *"Stupid Renner?"* And he would answer, *"Here!"* **He took on her opinion as his identity**.

Our rejection issues have deep roots.

The Principle of Roots

The Bible speaks of the principle of **roots**: Roots are things that are under the surface. They are usually hidden. However, roots that are under the surface determine what happens above the surface. Unhealthy roots will always produce unhealthy fruit!

Deuteronomy 29:18 NKJV Make sure there is no man or woman, clan or tribe among you today whose heart turns away from the Lord our God to go and worship the gods of those nations; make sure there is no root among you that produces such bitter poison.

Here, God says that the root of a heart turning away from the Lord will always produce a bitter poison that will bring outward destructive effects.

Hosea 9:16 NKJV Ephraim is blighted, their root is withered, they yield no fruit. Even if they bear children, I will slay their cherished offspring.

In this text, God points out that withered, or unhealthy roots cannot produce good fruit.

Hebrews 12:15 NLT Look after each other so that none of you fails to receive the grace of God. Watch out that no poisonous root of bitterness grows up to trouble you, corrupting many.

Roots of the Past

Every person is in some way the product of their past – in both good and bad ways. If their past was good and healthy, then the past produces lasting fruit that blesses their lives. But if their past was not good and was unhealthy, then the past produces lasting fruit in their lives that is unhealthy. People thinking, feeling, and reacting in unhealthy ways today are the fruit of an unhealthy past. Some of the unhealthy fruits of the past include ways of thinking, destructive emotions, addictions and relational difficulties.

- **Embarrassment and shame:** I have seen people talk or even think of their past – and even years later, they turn red with embarrassment or shame.
- **Anger:** Others become angry over events that may have happened years before. The events of the past still affect their emotions years later.
- **Fighting the past:** Some people live their lives reacting against past events. They may make internal vows such as, *"I will never let myself be put in that kind of situation again."* Or some spend their lives trying to prove people in their past wrong: *"I'll show them I'm not stupid. I'll prove that I'm not worthless."*

The roots of an unhealthy past prevent us from producing good things in our lives. This often manifests in an inability to form good relationships: *With God, and with other people.*

The past is not an <u>excuse</u>, it is an <u>explanation</u>. An incorrect response is to think a negative past gives us a free pass on needing to change or excuses us from treating people incorrectly.

2 Kings 2:19-22 NKJV [19]*Then the men of the city said to Elisha, "Please notice, the situation of this city is pleasant, as my lord sees;*

but the water is bad, and the ground barren." ²⁰And he said, "Bring me a new bowl, and put salt in it." So they brought it to him. ²¹Then he went out to the source of the water, and cast in the salt there, and said, ""Thus says the Lord: 'I have healed this water; from it there shall be no more death or barrenness.'" ²²So the water remains healed to this day, according to the word of Elisha which he spoke.

This story correctly explains how to heal from a negative past. The men of the city told him the negative history of the water, so Elisha knew <u>where</u> to apply supernatural healing!

CHAPTER 1 —— KEY 🔑 UNDERSTANDING

The past is not an excuse, it is an explanation.

Why the Past Has Effect Today

When thinking about the effects of negative roots in the past - the question is **why?** We can see that some things from the past do not affect us today. You may have broken your arm or suffered a cut somewhere in your body when you were young – but those cuts and injuries have no lasting effect today. They hurt at the time – but then they healed, and the effect is over. So why do some words or events from the past still have such a powerful effect on us today?

The answer is that there are God-created <u>needs</u> inside every person:

• God has designed every person to need relationships:

Genesis 2:18 NKJV *The Lord God said, "It is not good for the man to be alone. I will make a helper suitable for him."*

The phrase' helper suitable' actually means 'helper completing.' We are <u>incomplete</u> without human relationships. Healthy human relationships are supposed to supply some things you <u>have to have</u> in order to be healthy.

- **God has designed every person to need love and acceptance:** We must feel loved and accepted by the people in our lives. This isn't optional—it is a God-given need that affects every area of our lives.
- **<u>It affects your sense of worth</u>:** This means how you see your own value. R.C. Sproul said, *"We yearn to believe that in some way we are important. This inner drive is as intense as our need for water and oxygen."*
- **<u>It affects your identity</u>:** Identity is who you are – or who you're supposed to be. Have you ever known people who change their image all the time? At one time, they dress like an athlete; then they have a gangster rapper image, and then they look like a cowboy. It's not just that their interests have changed – **the problem is they don't know who they are!** Identity comes from within – but people try to adopt an identity from the outside. A young man in our church in South Africa asked me, *"Who am I?"* He wasn't talking about his name – he was expressing a lack of identity.
- **<u>It affects your security</u>:** Why do young children cling to their mother or father when nervous or frightened? Because they feel a measure of security. Love makes you feel safe. It is common for people to try to put on a particular face or image outside the home, but they think they can be themselves at home. We do this because we usually feel secure in our relationships in the home. Our family knows us, loves us, and accepts us.

The choices we make in life are made based on our self-worth and our identity. A Pastor tells a story of visiting a man in the hospital who was dying of AIDS. The man confessed that he was molested as a young boy. He said he always believed something was wrong with him and that he could never be like any men he admired. He said, *"I didn't want to be this way! I hate it! I hate myself! But this is who I am! This is how I see myself."*

That is why some past events have such a powerful effect on us even today. It's not that the event (rejection) is so powerful: It may have simply been a word spoken or a despising sneer. But the event was so powerful because our need for love and acceptance is so strong that it amplified the effects of rejection.

A family in our church was listening to me preach when the young daughter leaned over to her mother and said, *"Pastor Greg just said a bad word."* What was the bad word Pastor Greg said? **Stupid!** I had probably made a comment about sin being stupid. To me, stupid is just a six-letter word that is a description. To me, stupid is not a bad word – because I never had people attack me using that word. But to the parents who had been called 'stupid' when they were young – stupid is like an offensive curse word and is banned from their house. There are people that a mere word can cause pain because they were given a painful message somewhere in their past using that word.

Sometimes, we need to identify the unhealthy roots in our past – so we can uproot the adverse effects they are still producing in our lives today.

CHAPTER 1 —— KEY UNDERSTANDING

The choices we make in life are made based on our self-worth and our identity.

Roots Of Rejection

If it's true that our God-created need is for love and acceptance, then a powerful strategy of hell against us is to cause us to be **rejected** by people. **Rejection:** *To refuse to accept or approve; To fail to value - or fail to give value.*

Rejection most often comes through people:

Some people experience <u>active</u> rejection: Active rejection is intentional actions carried out in spoken words and physical actions against us.

Judges 11:2 NLT Gilead's wife also had several sons, and when these half brothers grew up, they chased Jephthah off the land. "You will not get any of our father's inheritance," they said, "for you are the son of a prostitute."
Even though they had the same father, the brothers told Jephthah, *"We do not want you here! You don't fit in our family. You have no right to have a place in our family."* They rejected him.

- Abandonment is active rejection.
- Divorce is active rejection.

  - Some divorces are caused by a parent who wants a new life – without their children.
  - A spouse who divorces you is actively rejecting you.
- Being told you are worthless, or stupid is active rejection.
- Being told you were not wanted is active rejection.

The Devil is a strategist. *He makes plans to cause us harm* and ensures that at specific points in our lives, we encounter someone who actively rejects us. Some people describe a point in life when a coach or teacher seemed to take an active dislike against them (not necessarily connected to their wrongdoing) or seemed to delight in making them feel bad.

I was raised with excellent, loving parents. But at a crucial moment in my teen years, the Devil inspired some men to go out of their way to belittle and torment me in various ways. I couldn't work out what I was doing wrong to deserve this. I didn't realize at the time this was a strategy of hell to attack my confidence, my identity, and to put a fear of rejection into me.

Some people experience <u>passive</u> rejection: *Passive rejection is a failure to give what is needed: Love and acceptance.*
For some this was shown in emotional coldness, or a lack of communication: *never being shown affection or words of love and acceptance.* A common statement people say is, *"I'm sure my father or mother loved me – they just never said it."*

Genesis 27:38 NKJV *Esau said to his father, "Do you have only one blessing, my father? Bless me too, my father!" Then Esau wept aloud.*

The book "The Impossible Climb" tells of a time when Ben Smalley visited his friend Alex Honnhold and grew concerned

about the way his friend was handling the death of his father, which was to act as though nothing had happened. Smalley said, *"I remember explicitly asking him, 'Why aren't you grieving more?'"* Alex explained it away, telling Smalley, *"Dad and I weren't super close. All he really did was take me climbing—it's all we shared. We didn't talk. He just sort of ghosted through the house. It's hard to miss someone who wasn't really there."*

Rejection can come through events or circumstances:

- The death of a parent when a child is young changes how they view the world and instills fear into their hearts and minds.
- Physical or sexual abuse gives a terrible message to those who have been abused.
- Failure makes people feel rejected. Failure is common to every human being – it's simply not possible to win every time in life. However, people who have failed at school, in business, or in ministry attach an incorrect value message to the perceived failure.
- People born into poverty often feel rejected. When they go to school, they see classmates with clothes or toys they can't afford. They incorrectly interpret this as, *"I don't have worth,"* or, *"My value comes from what I own."*

The Fruit of Rejection

The roots of rejection always produce fruit: *negative, destructive effects in our lives.* This is because every rejection carries a message about ourselves—and the message is a lie!
The Devil's main weapon he uses against us is **lies.** *He is a liar!*

> **John 8:44 NCV** *You belong to your father the devil, and you want to do what he wants. He was a murderer from the beginning*

and was against the truth, because there is no truth in him. When he tells a lie, he shows what he is really like, because he is a liar and the father of lies.

The message we receive from every rejection is a lie about our worth:

- I have no worth – that is why I was rejected.
- My worth is based on other people's opinions of me.
- My worth is based on how I perform.

- My worth is based on my looks or my body.
- My worth is based on sexuality.
- My worth is based on what I own.

These lies produce destructive fruits.

Romans 8:15 NCV The Spirit we received does not make us slaves again to fear; it makes us children of God. With that Spirit we cry out, "Father."

For rejected people – fear is a predominant mindset:

- We fear being worthless.
- We fear being rejected.
- We fear relationships.
- We fear failure.
- We fear commitment.
- We fear GOD!

Rejection becomes a <u>mindset</u> that filters every word we hear, every action people around us take, and every situation we encounter - and it dominates our lives.

2 Corinthians 10:4 NKJV For the weapons of our warfare are not carnal but mighty in God for pulling down strongholds.
The word <u>stronghold</u> has two distinct word meanings:
1. Prison: People are trapped or held captive in unhealthy ways of thinking, acting, and reacting.
2. Fort: *A fort is a military outpost that dominates an area;* In olden times a fort was in a place that enabled the soldiers to determine the access to and from the area.

Many rejected people describe feeling uncomfortable with people, either individually or in crowds. They have nagging feelings that they don't belong or fear that they don't fit somehow. They sometimes have an urge to run away from people to escape that discomfort. They often don't know what the source of these feelings is—it is rejection!

Rejection isn't just psychological – it is supernatural.

2 Corinthians 10:4 NKJV Speaks of ""the weapons of our warfare." This is the same imagery and language used in ***Ephesians 6:12 NLT** For we are not fighting against flesh-and-blood enemies, but against evil rulers and authorities of the unseen world, against mighty powers in this dark world, and against evil spirits in the heavenly places.*

What creates strongholds of incorrect thinking? What traps people into patterns of destructive emotions, reactions, and decisions? Supernatural spirit beings that fight against us! **Rejection is a demonic spirit!** That is why therapy or information alone cannot fix it.

Rejection dominates our relationships with God and with people.

• Rejection prevents a healthy relationship with God.

- Rejection prevents healthy relationships with people.

Rejection dominates our view of ourselves.

Numbers 13:33 NKJV There we saw the giants (the descendants of Anak came from the giants); and we were like grasshoppers in our own sight, and so we were in their sight.

The result of centuries of rejection and violation by the Egyptians changed how God's people viewed themselves: We are like grasshoppers – we are unable to do what God wants us to do. But notice that was not how <u>God</u> viewed them! Rejection had given them a message that was a lie – and they now believed the enemy's lies about them.

Healing And Healthy Roots

We will talk later in the book specifically about how to uproot rejection from our lives, but for now I want to give you some hope: *God plans to bring deliverance and healing from the past!*

God wants to remove unhealthy roots that affect us today.

Jeremiah 31:28 NKJV And it shall come to pass, that as I have watched over them to pluck up, to break down, to throw down, to destroy, and to afflict, so I will watch over them to build and to plant, says the Lord.
Luke 17:6 NKJV And the Lord said, If ye had faith as a grain of mustard seed, ye might say unto this sycamine tree, Be thou plucked up by the root, and be thou planted in the sea; and it should obey you.

In both verses, God has the power to pluck up or uproot things. He will supernaturally enable His people to uproot unhealthy things in their own lives.

God wants to bring healing from the past.

Luke 4:18 NKJV The Spirit of the Lord is upon Me, Because He has anointed Me To preach the gospel to the poor; He has sent Me to heal the brokenhearted, To proclaim liberty to the captives And recovery of sight to the blind, To set at liberty those who are oppressed;

The answer to anything negative at work in our lives is a miracle of healing.
- The healing of our lives begins in our hearts.

   He has sent Me to heal the brokenhearted...
- The result of healing is liberty – or freedom.

   To proclaim liberty to the captives... To set at liberty those who are oppressed;

God wants to plant healthy roots in our hearts & minds.

Psalm 1:3 NKJV He is like a tree planted by streams of water, which yields its fruit in season and whose leaf does not wither. Whatever he does prospers.

If the unhealthy roots in our lives are based on lies, the healthy roots God plants within us are based on truth.

   Psalm 43:3 NKJV Oh, send out Your light and Your truth! Let them lead me; Let them bring me to Your holy hill And to Your tabernacle.

Chris Thorne
Mom left & Foster Care

God shines light into the darkness of our hearts – the lies that we have believed that come from rejection. He shows us the truth from His word – which brings us into His presence. That is the basis of a healthy relationship with God. When that happens, it will affect every area of our lives.

Testimony: Good afternoon, Pastor Greg. I wanted to send you a quick email on behalf of my Church to say how thankful we are for the series on rejection that you are doing. I got saved as a teenager, and for many years, I struggled with feelings of being unwanted and a lack of acceptance, especially when I would visit some of the other Churches here in the UK. When you mentioned the root of these feelings was a spirit of rejection, I realized you were describing me! I told my Pastor that I had been watching the series at home, and he decided to show it to the Church on Sunday evenings. It has greatly helped and blessed the people. Those who wouldn't normally open up about their struggles are now beginning to share them so they can find freedom. Thank you so much for the series.

Leebon Britoe
Mother died

Prayer: As you begin this book, I'm going to pray now that God will help you as you continue to read or listen, and I'm going to ask God to do a miracle in you.

God, every person that has taken the time they're reading, they're listening. Or maybe they're watching this right now. I need You to open the eyes of their understanding. God, they're going to see things in this book that will open their eyes to things in the past.

Greg Mitchell
Chapter 1 - Roots of Rejection

And I'm asking You to guide them through this journey so that they can find healing. God, I pray that You will open the eyes of their understanding. That they are going to get a correct view of who You are, and You are able to bring healing. God, I pray that You're going to use this book. Touch them and bring a miracle of deliverance in Jesus' name. Amen.

Chapter 2
Rejection and the Home
Part 1

Rabbi Shmuley Boteach was friends with Michael Jackson for several years. He said, *"I think Michael lived with a profound fear of rejection."* He said Michael told him that, *"Everything I've done in pursuing fame, in honing my craft was an effort to be loved because I never felt loved."* He also said, *"I lived for my father's approval and acceptance."*

The example of Michael Jackson shows the profound impact the home has in implanting roots of rejection.

God's Design of Family

God has designed the family to be the foundation of human relationships and personality.

The family – the home is meant to be a place of acceptance.

Have you seen parents who believe their baby is the most beautiful child in the world? *(Even when they clearly are not!)* That is good! God made parents to be that way – so they would value and communicate that value to their child.

We see young children run to and cling to their parents when they are nervous or scared. The child is not sure about the stranger in front of them, but they instinctively feel a parent accepts them. The home is the starting place of acceptance: The primary place of acceptance in life.

In a perfect world – this is what a family should be:

- There should be both a Father and a Mother.
    - The Book of Genesis (Beginnings) shows us God's blueprint for family: He created Adam and Eve to be the first parents: *A biological man and a biological woman!*
- The parents should <u>want</u> the child they created.
- The parents should <u>raise</u> the children.
    - Raising children involves **Presence** (being there), **Provision** (supplying what is needed in life), and **Instruction** (teaching what the child needs to know in life – every area).
- The parents should love the children with *words, affection, and actions.*
- The parents should accept the child unconditionally:
    - Love is not based on performance. They do not make comments such as, *"I love you if you achieve. I love you if you never make a mistake."*

When these are present in a healthy family - they provide powerful things inside a person:

- **Identity**: *Who you are.*
- **Confidence**: *Confidence is how you see yourself - based on your worth or your value.*
    - Children who are raised in a healthy atmosphere in the home that communicates love and acceptance often exhibit confidence in life.
- **Reference points**: *What am I supposed to do in life – what am I supposed to be?*

- I learned how to value women, how to show love to my wife, and how to treat people in my parents' home!
- **Boundaries:** *How much is too far in life? What is unacceptable behavior?*
  - These should be learned first in the home.

Rejection in The Home

God's plan of love and acceptance is not what many people experience in their lives:

The home can be the place of life's first rejections and the place where we experience the greatest rejections of our lives.

> ***Psalm 27:10 NLT*** *Even if my father and mother abandon me, the Lord will hold me close.*

The Bible tells many stories of family rejection: *Because it is so common.*

- Jacob experienced rejection by his Father: *He blatantly preferred his brother over him.*
- Joseph was rejected by his own brothers: *Their envy made them work against him.*
- David was rejected by his Father: *When God said one of his sons would become King, he didn't even ask David to be there; He thought David was only good for taking care of sheep – not leadership!*
- David was rejected by his brother Eliab: *His brother doubted his ability and attacked his motives for wanting to do something good.*
- Jesus was rejected by His own family
  - ***John 7:5 NKJV*** *For even His brothers did not believe in Him.*

UNDERSTANDING

The home can be the place of life's first rejections and the place where we experience the greatest rejections of our lives.

Let's look at some of the many ways rejection can come to us in the home:

Rejection comes from our birth circumstances: *For some reason - the birth was not wanted.*

- This can be because of an unwanted pregnancy: For many reasons!
    - The mother's age when she falls pregnant: *She feels she is too young or too old.*
    - The child was the result of an affair, incest, or rape.
    - The child will negatively impact the parent's finances, or life plans.
        Research has shown that being unwanted is actually felt by the baby in the womb!
    - Disappointment over the child's sex:
    Perhaps the father says I wanted a boy – when the baby is a girl. Or the mother says I hate men – and the baby is a boy.

There can be Inherited rejection: *Parents with a root of rejection pass it on spiritually and literally.*

- There is a spiritual transfer of a family curse: *Evil spirits gain entrance to the children.*
- Rejected parents often recreate in their children the same rejection they experienced.

I suggest that you have mercy on your parents: *They often didn't know any better because of how they were raised!*

Rejection comes by abandonment: *A parent that leaves the children.*

An epidemic crisis in our society is men who won't raise the child they created after pregnancy occurs. It is increasingly common for children to never be raised by their biological fathers. Many people have never met their biological Father or don't even know who he is!

Sometimes, parents run away and abandon their family at some point in a child's life.

- **This can be because of stress:** One parent says, *"I can't cope with the stress of marriage and parenting,"* so they run away to relieve their stress. But they do not consider the stress this brings to the children.

- **This can be because of selfishness:** A parent who wants to live as though they have no responsibilities will sometimes abandon their children so they can play, party, or pursue their own selfish interests.

- **This can be because of an affair:** The fantasy of an illicit sexual affair can cause a parent to lose all common sense and abandon their children to pursue a fantasy romance.
2 Timothy 3:3 NKJV (a mark of the last days is that people will be) without natural affection.

- **This can be because of divorce:** *Increasingly in our world, when couples are having problems in their marriage, they don't choose to <u>work</u> it out – they choose to <u>get</u> out!*

The great tragedy of divorce is the potential damage to the children.

Malachi 2:16 NKJV *"For the LORD God of Israel says That He hates divorce, For it covers one's garment with violence," Says the LORD of hosts. Therefore take heed to your spirit, That you do not deal treacherously."*

- **Divorce does violent damage to a child's security.**
- **Divorce does violent damage to a child's identity.**
- **Divorce does violent damage to a child's financial provision.**
- **Divorce does violent damage to a child's sense of responsibility.**

The tragic consequence of divorce is that the children often interpret their parent's divorce as being their fault. They can think, *"If I was a better son or daughter, my parents would not have divorced. They divorced because they didn't want me."*

Writer/Director Karen Moncrieff speaks about the effect her parent's divorce had on her. She says, *"You end up searching for surrogate fathers who will approve of you."*

Rejection comes through the addictions of parents: *Such as alcohol, drugs, or pornography.*

- A heavily addicted parent can be so absorbed with their addiction, they fail to give their children the love, affection, time, and attention they need.
- Addictions create instability in the home.
  - Financial instability as they lose jobs or spend income on their addiction instead of paying bills to provide for their family.
  - Relational instability as parents fight over the effects of the addiction.

- Addictions give children the message that the drug, alcohol, or pornography has more value than their child.

I read of a Rapper who described his childhood: He said, *"My drug addict father would say he was going to pick me up to spend time with me, but then he wouldn't show up – he was addicted to drugs. HE CHOSE DRUGS OVER ME – HE LOVED DRUGS MORE THAN ME!"*

Rejection comes through abuse: Abuse can be physical violence, verbal abuse, or sexual abuse.
- Abuse can come as people lose control due to alcohol or drugs.

    I've had people tell me that while growing up, a parent treated them good when they were sober, but when drunk or high, they would become violent and abusive.

Such children lack all security in life. Your world can be turned upside down in a moment.
- Sadly, some twisted people enjoy hurting children. That is unthinkable.
- Abuse is an assault on your sense of worth:
  - A child thinks, *"I must not be good – if they treat me this way."*
  - Sexual abuse gives a false and twisted message of your worth: *That somehow you are only good for sex.*

If you believe that lie, you come to believe the lie that my identity is sexuality.

Rejection comes by harsh words: *Harsh words are an overflow of what's going on in their parent's lives.*

- Some harsh words are a reaction to a child's mistakes or lack of performance:
  - *What good are you? You're stupid. You're worthless.*

    Perhaps a parent reacts like this because <u>they</u> lack self-worth. They want the child to perform well (or perfectly) as this will give <u>them</u> a sense of worth.

- Some harsh words are a reaction to their own frustration and pain in life.
  - *I hate you. I never wanted you. I wish you were never born. I wish I aborted you.*

I was trying to understand why a man seemed to hate himself and could not receive love. I asked, *"Where did this start?"* He told me, *"When I was young, my mother would tell me how much she hated me and wished I was never born. She would do this while threatening to kill all the children and herself."*

Rejection comes by withholding love:

Love must be expressed through words of love, acceptance, and approval. Unfortunately, some people have never heard such words said to them by their parents.

Love is meant to be expressed in non-sexual, physical ways:

Luke 15:20 NCV So the son left and went to his father. "While the son was still a long way off, his father saw him and felt sorry for his son. So the father ran to him and hugged and kissed him."

Many parents do not physically demonstrate love for their children.

This is a God-given need inside people – to receive love in non-sexual, physical ways – such as a hug, a kiss, a pat on the head, or a pat on the back. When this is absent, children are vulnerable to the first person who will express love and affection through physical touch. Unfortunately, this is usually sexual – and creates many problems.

Rejection comes through an inability to show attention or give time:

- They are not being actively abusive – just failing to give their child the attention love requires.
  - I've had numerous people describe a parent, "They were sort of just there."
  - They never spoke to or interacted with their children.
- The message inattention conveys is, "You are not worth my time or attention."

Rejection comes through parents who are demanding or hard to please:

- Some parent's love is performance based.

  They say, "*I will love and accept you if you do right. If you win. If you succeed.*" But this is a big problem; *We don't always do right, win, or succeed...so what then?*

- Some children can never do enough to please their parents.

  They have ridiculously high standards: They almost want perfection. *I read of a young man who came in 2nd place in a state-wide track meet. That is quite an accomplishment, but afterwards his dad said to him, ""How does it feel to be the first loser?"*

Rejection comes through favoritism:

- This describes when a parent blatantly prefers a sibling:

  They may say, "Why can't you be like your sister? Why can't you be like your brother?"

  Jacob and Esau experienced chaos in the home because each parent (Isaac and Rebekah) had a favorite. Isaac preferred Esau, and Rebekah preferred Jacob.
- Parents can even actively encourage sibling rivalry and competition.

They mistakenly think it will help the children succeed and get ahead in life!

All of these experiences in the home produce rejection: *To fail to value - or fail to give value.*

- Rejection can be defined as a profound sense of being unwanted.
  - *The word rejection means to be cast aside and thrown away as having no value.*
- Rejection gives you the message: *You have no value. You don't fit. You don't measure up. Something is wrong with you.*

The Lies of Rejection

The greatest danger of rejection is that rejection tells us lies.

- The Devil's greatest strategy is to get us to believe lies!

John 8:44 NIV You belong to your father, the devil, and you want to carry out your father's desire. He was a murderer from the beginning, not holding to the truth, for there is no truth in him. When he lies, he speaks his native language, for he is a liar and the father of lies.

Eve's life was forever changed when she believed the lies the serpent told her!

Look at some of the lies rejection gets us to believe:

- You have no worth: *I obviously have no worth if people treated me like that.*
- It's your fault: *Your parent left you. Your parents divorced. You were abused.*

If you were a better child, they wouldn't have done that.

People live with an overall feeling of guilt: *I don't deserve good. I deserve bad things.*

My wife and I knew a man who obviously suffered this kind of guilt. He worked hard, and his income enabled him to buy clothes or sunglasses he wanted or needed. But periodically, his roommates would find that he had thrown all his clothes or sunglasses in the trash because he felt guilty that he had anything good. They would have to rescue his things out of the bin.

- Your worth is based on performance: *I only deserve love if I perform well or do right.*
- You need to be perfect: *I can only prevent people from rejecting me again if I am perfect.*
- Everyone in life will reject you like your parents did: *That is a fear-based lie!*

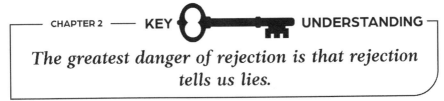

CHAPTER 2 —— KEY UNDERSTANDING

The greatest danger of rejection is that rejection tells us lies.

The Primary Result of Rejection is an Inability to Receive or Communicate Love.

Human relationships:

- Some people struggle with communication because of the rejection they have experienced.
  - They struggle with telling people they love them or how they feel about them.
  - They feel love for others – but they struggle to say it.
  - They believe you shouldn't ever let people know what's going on inside you:

They think people might reject them if they knew they had problems.

- Some people struggle with affection because of the rejection they have experienced.
  - Receiving affection: They think, *"Don't touch me! It's sexual."*
  - Giving affection: They feel awkward giving a hug, a pat on the back, or a kiss.

In our family, affection was as normal as breathing. We say it, and we show it. My wife wasn't raised like that. It took some adjusting on her part to get used to giving and receiving affection.

- Gifts: They don't like getting gifts. They think, *"I don't want to feel like I owe you anything."*

Relationship with God: Unfortunately, we transfer our feelings toward our parents onto God.

- For very rejected people, when they get saved, they hear that God is a Father.

  But to them – that is not good news: *You mean like my cold, abandoning, abusive father?*
- The opposite of love is not hate – it is fear:

1 John 4:18 NKJV *There is no fear in love; but perfect love casts out fear, because fear involves torment. But he who fears has not been made perfect in love.*

- People can be saved – yet they live in fear in their relationship with God.
  - I'm afraid God can't be trusted: He will let me down – like my parents.
  - I'm afraid I don't measure up in God's eyes:
    He may give up on me when He sees what I'm like
- I must perform to deserve or earn God's love.

In Jesus' story of the prodigal son in Luke 15. The Elder Brother struggled with feelings of rejection in the home. He felt rejected by his father.

Luke 15:29-30 NIV 29But he answered his father, Look! All these years I've been slaving for you and never disobeyed your orders. Yet you never gave me even a young goat so I could celebrate with my friends. 30But when this son of yours who has squandered your property with prostitutes comes home, you kill the fattened calf for him!'

There are far too many Elder-Brother Christians. They are doing the right actions, but their motivation in doing them is so the Father will love them.

Luke 15:31 NIV 'My son,' the father said, 'you are always with me, and everything I have is yours.'

Everything has always been yours! You have always had a wonderful inheritance in your father's house! The tragedy is that rejected, Elder-Brother Christians are trying to earn something that has always been theirs!

CHAPTER 2 —— KEY UNDERSTANDING

The Primary Result of Rejection is an Inability to Receive or Communicate Love.

Testimony: When Pastor Greg announced that he would begin a Sunday School series on rejection, I remember thinking this would not apply to me. Since I grew up with both parents and in a stable, Christian home and loving environment, I assumed that rejection could not have influenced my life. However, in the lessons, Pastor Greg described acute indicators of how rejection plays out in a life. I would find myself saying, "Wait a minute, that's what I do; that's how I think." I quickly discovered that rejection doesn't have to be blatant for one to experience rejection. Simply accepting the lies of Satan is enough to cultivate roots of rejection.

I spent years of my life seeking acceptance of the opposite sex. This drove me to destructive behavior patterns. I had to know: Do they like me, do they find me attractive, do they want me? If a pretty girl accepted, liked, or showed me attention, my sense of self-worth was validated - but only temporarily.

I had a childhood crush on a girl. Though I was only around nine years old, I did everything to win her attention: gifts, songs, letters, and kind words. She finally told me to leave her alone because her older brother would tease her. This didn't just produce temporary embarrassment, sadness, and shame; her rejection affected my view of myself. Why didn't she like me? What was wrong with me? Her innocent plea to be left alone was not a reflection of my masculinity, looks, or desirability. We were just kids, but it sent a message that stuck.

As I got older, I developed an unhealthy desire to be accepted by women. This did not end at the dating phase. It carried well into marriage. I craved female attention and validation and never understood why this was so important to me. I didn't need a therapist or a reconciliation with my childhood crush; I needed deliverance from rejection and to crush the lie. I do not attribute all my rejection to this one childhood event. There were many other events in my life that did damage to my self-esteem and view of women. However, in childhood, we are very impressionable, and the enemy wastes no time planting the seeds of rejection that can affect us for our entire lives if we fail to identify and uproot them. I so appreciate that I found healing in this area of my life and others. Uprooting rejection corrected the way I viewed the women and myself.

Leebon Britoe
Aunt put that on us

Greg Mitchell
Chapter 2 - Rejection and Home - Part 1

Prayer: Now that you finished this chapter about the rejection in the home, I want to pray for you that God is going to help you in this process of healing from rejection that has come through your events in the home. God, I pray that You're going to help people. I'm asking that You open their eyes. There are events that happened in their homes that have implanted roots of rejection. Some of these things are very painful for people. I need You even now to begin to apply the healing oil of the Holy Spirit into broken hearts. I'm asking that now. God, You're going to begin that process of pulling up those roots from their hearts. Bring healing and deliverance as they continue through the book. Let them find a miracle of healing and identity in You, God, and begin to do that right now in the name of Jesus Christ. I thank You. Amen.

Chapter 3
Rejection and the Home
Part 2

Rejection Infection

In 1906, Mary Mallon got a job as a cook with a wealthy New York family. She went with the family when they rented a house for the summer. That summer, six out of eleven people in the house came down with Typhoid Fever. After an investigation, authorities found that Mary was an asymptomatic carrier of the bacteria that causes Typhoid. Investigators discovered that she worked for twelve different families, and all of them had outbreaks of Typhoid Fever during her employment. One hundred twenty-two people total were infected by contact with her, and five people died. She was dubbed "Typhoid Mary" by the Press. She carried a deadly disease within her body – and unknowingly transmitted it into the homes where she lived and worked.

This is true of the Spirit of Rejection: Those who have suffered rejection in various ways become carriers of that Spirit – and transmit it to others in their homes. There are three reasons for this unhealthy spiritual transmission:

An inherited curse: Evil spirits gain entrance to families – and are passed on to children.

> *Exodus 34:7 NKJV ...visiting the iniquity of the fathers upon the children and the children's children to the third and the fourth generation.*

This speaks of evil supernatural influence: *It is <u>unseen</u> – but it has an <u>effect.</u>* People reproduce the negative traits of their family – even if they hate it! These spirits drive people to act in unhealthy ways. Rejection is like this: A spirit transferred into us drives us to act in unhealthy ways. Unfortunately, the people on the receiving end of this spirit – are our families.

An example that was set: *Much unhealthy behavior is learned by example.*

In the Bible, we see that Isaac used deception to save himself – at the expense of his wife. But that is what he saw his father Abraham do: *He learned it by example.* Rejection causes parents to treat others incorrectly. *But that teaches children how to act.* A man tells of his experience growing up: Whenever his parents argued, one of them would grab a plate and smash it. Later, when he got married, he and his wife had their first argument, and he grabbed a plate and smashed it. He realized, *"I did that – just like my parents!"*

Emotions that dominate: *People take actions based on their emotions.*

Rejection produces negative emotions, *and those emotions cause us to act incorrectly.* Angry people often cause pain to others. People who feel a lack of worth will fight any perceived insult to their worth.

Rejection At Work in The Home

The danger of rejection is that the past pain can become present in our homes and family. Look at some of the ways that pain manifests in the home.

Anger and resentment: Rejection & violations cause emotional pain – and pain produces anger.

Hebrews 12:15 NIV See to it that no one misses the grace of God and that no bitter root grows up to cause trouble and defile many.

The word 'bitter' means something sharp – something that pokes you and causes pain. Rejection causes pain that keeps on hurting – years after the event of rejection is over. I have seen people weep over events that happened many years ago.

The word 'defile' means stained or ruined. The text says that bitterness 'defiles many.' Other people feel the effects of your bitterness. *Is it possible that you are angry at someone from the past – and taking it out on people in the present?*

2 Samuel 6:16 NIV Now as the ark of the Lord came into the City of David, Michal, Saul's daughter, looked through a window and saw King David leaping and whirling before the Lord; and she despised him in her heart.

Michal's father mistreated her by trying to kill her husband: *He accused her of disloyalty.* But then she looked at her husband David incorrectly and mistreated him. *Her pain distorted her vision and motivated her to cause her husband pain.*

A Pastor told me of a young man in his church who was constantly getting into conflicts with various people in the church. He brought him into the office to try to speak to him about this. The man suddenly started angrily yelling at the Pastor, then jumped up and ran out of the office. The Pastor was about to go after the man, when God spoke to him and said, *"Don't go after him. He's not talking to you. He's talking to his father."*

32

Is it possible that you are angry at someone from the past – and taking it out on people in the present?

Interpretation: When something is damaged inside us – it affects how we <u>see</u> things.

>**Titus 1:15 NLT** *Everything is pure to those whose hearts are pure. But nothing is pure to those who are corrupt and unbelieving, because their minds and consciences are corrupted.*

When rejection takes root – we see and hear things incorrectly: *With a false message.* We see and hear everything with the message of worth or value, even when it has nothing to do with our worth or value.

A wife can ask her husband a simple question: *"Why didn't you take out the trash?"* But the husband responds, *"So you're saying I'm stupid!"* She was asking a simple question about trash. But what he <u>heard</u> was an attack on his <u>intelligence</u> – an attack on his <u>worth</u>! The husband misinterprets her words because of a spirit of rejection within him. This problem of interpretation occurs in many marriage conflicts. One spouse will tell the other of an issue that is bothering them. *"I don't like when you say that to me, or It hurts me when you do that."* That is information. But, often, the response from the other spouse is, *"So, you hate me!"*

The result is that many couples don't fight about <u>issues</u> – they fight over <u>feelings</u>, and those feelings are based on lies that rejection has imparted to us.

Re-creation: Without God – people tend to reproduce their past.

The old cliché is true: 'Hurt people - hurt people.' Abused people can become abusive. People who have been damaged by hateful words tend to pass that on to their spouse and their children!
People raised with coldness and lack of communication tend to reproduce that.

> **Genesis NIV 4:23-24** *Lamech said to his wives, "Adah and Zillah, listen to me; wives of Lamech, hear my words. I have killed a man for wounding me, a young man for injuring me. 24If Cain is avenged seven times, then Lamech seventy-seven times."*

Correction Without Balance

It is a simple fact of parenting that children need correction. They will do wrong, because the Bible says in **Proverbs 22:15 NKJV** *Foolishness is in the heart of a child*...that's just a fact.

The answer to foolishness is correction (some translations say discipline):

> **Proverbs 22:15 NCV** *Every child is full of foolishness, but punishment can get rid of it.*

The problem is when the parents doing the correction or discipline suffer from the effects of rejection and have a spirit of rejection driving them. They will misinterpret their children's wrong behavior, which causes them to view or administer correction without balance.

Rejected Parents can tend to view correction through the lens of self-worth: *You're making me look bad!* They are concerned about the child's behavior <u>primarily</u> because they are concerned about how other people will view <u>them</u>! If you view your child this way, you can tend to be excessive in correction. I see parents who insist that their child not move a muscle or breathe! *But they are children, not robots!* My question to such parents is, *"Are you doing that for the <u>child</u> – or for <u>you</u>?"*

Rejected parents can also bring correction without hope. Parents who view their children's behavior as a vote on their self-worth tend to be like this. When their child does wrong, they are shocked. *How could you?* (Because they are human!) Therefore, they give correction without hope:

- They refuse to speak to their child for days or weeks.
- They remind them of their failure again and again.

Depending on the severity of the violation or sin of the child, I have known parents that cut off their relationship with their child completely – and never have a relationship again!

This is true for Christian parents who have backslidden children. A child choosing to leave God and turn to sin is heartbreaking on many levels. I know this from personal experience. You grieve for lost potential. You are worried about potential damage. You are concerned for their soul in eternity.

But when you add your own rejection to this, you make the difficult situation much harder than it should be. You make the <u>child's</u> sin be about <u>your</u> worth. *What will people think of us? You have shamed the family!*

I have tried to bring balance to grieving parents: I ask them, *"You didn't teach them to sin, tell them to sin, or say it was okay to sin, correct?"* They will say no. *"Then why are you making their* sin be *your* fault – or your shame?" That is an imbalanced view.

Hope For the Home

Let me give good news to anyone who feels the damage of rejection: **You are not doomed by your past!** It is a mistake to think that because you were rejected, you can never get over it – or you will somehow be less than others.

> *1 Chronicles 4:9-10 NIV Now Jabez was more honorable than his brothers, and his mother called his name Jabez, saying, "Because I bore him in pain." ¹⁰And Jabez called on the God of Israel saying, "Oh, that You would bless me indeed, and enlarge my territory, that Your hand would be with me, and that You would keep me from evil, that I may not cause pain!" So God granted him what he requested.*

Jabez didn't look to people to overcome the pain of his past: *He took it to God.*

CHAPTER 3 —— **KEY** **UNDERSTANDING**

You are not doomed by your past!

The answer for rejection is not people – it is <u>God</u>!

Some people think: *If I could find the people who rejected me, get them to apologize, get them to say they love me...it would fix me!* But that is not true.

> *Psalm 27:10 NLT Even if my father and mother abandon me, the Lord will hold me close.*

Only God can heal the wounds of rejection.

Matthew 12:13 NKJV Then He said to the man, "Stretch out your hand." And he stretched it out, and it was restored as whole as the other.

His hand was made <u>whole</u>: *Healed and functioning as God intended it.* God can not only do that with physical bodies, He can make our hearts whole: *Healed and functioning as God intended it.*

Healing Your Home

We must ensure that we break the curse of rejection in our own homes. This is a powerful part of salvation: **Break the demonic curses that are at work in families!**

Galatians 3:13-14 NIV Christ redeemed us from the curse of the law by becoming a curse for us, for it is written: "Cursed is everyone who is hung on a tree." [14]He redeemed us in order that the blessing given to Abraham might come to the Gentiles through Christ Jesus, so that by faith we might receive the promise of the Spirit.

You break the curse supernaturally:
We first <u>recognize</u> a curse at work in our family. The old saying is true: *The Devil exposed is the Devil defeated.*
Then we pray: *Cast out the spirits tormenting us – and close the door.*

You break the curse by personal decisions: *I will not pass on to my family what cursed my life!*
That is my parent's story: *Dad was born into poverty. His mother ran off with another man, leaving five children when Dad was five years old. He was raised by his father, who worked long hours and had addiction issues. His father had a heart attack*

& died in my Dad's arms. He went to live with his mother, who had previously abandoned the kids, but it didn't work. He tried to live with his sister and her husband, but it didn't work. He moved to Prescott and got a job in hotel that supplied a room, so he would have a place to live. He lived alone in the hotel for his final year of high school. My Mom had a distant relationship with her father. When they married, they could have passed on the same rejection they experienced to us kids. BUT THEY BROKE THE CURSE! They decided they were not going to live like that. So, we were raised with love, affection, affirmation, and acceptance. You would never know by the way they raised us that they had experienced rejection.

WAYMAN MITCHELL AND SIBLINGS

NELDA MITCHELL WITH HER DAD

NELDA MITCHELL   WAYMAN AND GREG MITCHELL

MITCHELL FAMILY - 1972

Look at raising children with blessing – instead of cursing with rejection:

Speak words of value: *Proverbs 18:21 NIV The tongue has the power of life and death, and those who love it will eat its fruit.*

Power comes through what is communicated! Love and acceptance must be spoken out loud, and they must be communicated to our children. Silence also speaks, but often, it is not what we intend to communicate. *You are not loved. You are not valued. You are not accepted by me.* We need to hear that we are valued.

> *Matthew 3:17 NIV And a voice from heaven said, "This is my Son, whom I love; with him I am well pleased."*

Children need to hear parents say words to their children, such as: *I love you. I'm proud of you. You did a good job. I'm glad you're my son, or I'm glad you're my daughter. You make me happy that you're mine. I will always love you.*

In the Bible, fathers such as Isaac and Jacob blessed their sons. The word bless means *to bow or to kneel:* You are attaching great importance to the one you bless.

Speak words of future blessing: Words give a picture of hope and future good.

> *Genesis 49:8 NKJV Judah, you are he whom your brothers shall praise; Your hand shall be on the neck of your enemies; Your father's children shall bow down before you.*

Parents can say things to their children, such as: *You're going to have a good future. God's going to help you. You are going to help people someday.* People often live up to the expectations of others, *so why not give expectations of good things?*

Give meaningful touch: Love & affection involves touching. *This is <u>not</u> sexual touching!*

Human touch is crucial: **People need it!** *A reporter interviewed Marilyn Monroe. Knowing that she had been shuffled from one foster home to another, she asked if Marilyn had ever felt loved by any of the families. With tears in her eyes, she replied, "Once, when I was about 7 or 8. The woman I was living with was putting on makeup while I watched. She was in a good mood, so she reached over and patted my cheeks. For that moment, I felt loved by her."*

> ***Genesis 48:10 KJV** Now the eyes of Israel were dim for age, so that he could not see. And he brought them near unto him; and he kissed them, and embraced them.*

Children <u>need</u> hugs, kisses, pats on the back, holding hands, pats on the head, etc. *Don't let some unhealthy boy or girl be the first one in their life to ever show them affection!*

Balance correction and affection: Children <u>will</u> do wrong! *Even your angel will do wrong!*

Connect your correction to their behavior, not their worth: When you have to correct them, tell them what they did that was wrong: *I'm punishing you for that, or I'm correcting you for that.*

The correction is simply issue-based! *Don't spit in your sister's food. Don't use the couch as a trampoline...* It should not be: *You stupid idiot! What kind of moron spits in people's food? I wish I never had you!*

Balance out your correction: After you bring correction, there will be emotions (tears), but then show your child affection and express your love for them. In my house, we were allowed to cry for a time after we were corrected. Then my Dad or Mom would say, *"Okay - now stop it! "* Then they would hug us and say, *"I love you."*

Don't connect <u>your</u> worth as a human being to your children's behavior. Children will do wrong things – because ***Proverbs 22:15 NKJV*** *Foolishness is in the heart of a child.* Even if you were the perfect parent, they will still do wrong things. If you are training them, correcting them, and setting a good example – their behavior is not a reflection of your worth.

Please don't hold the offense over their heads: Treat them normally once the correction is over. Don't refuse to speak to them or remind them of the offense repeatedly for hours, days, or weeks.

We had a man on staff named Josh Neal in Prescott as concert director. He had initially been saved in another church where his Pastor was abusive and cruel. He did well on staff, and we sent the Neals out to Pastor in Blythe, CA. Just before Josh left, I asked him what was different about being in our church than the church he was initially saved in. He said, *"When I was on staff if I made a mistake, you would tell me what I did wrong and rebuke me. Then, minutes later, you treated me completely normally. You didn't hold it against me or continue to punish me for what I did wrong."* He said if he made a mistake in his original church, the Pastor wouldn't speak to him for days or weeks.

Unfortunately, that is how some parents treat their children when they correct them. That is a mistake! You are changing the message from **'you <u>did</u> bad'** to **'you <u>are</u> bad.'** The first approach (you did bad) corrects behavior and trains them for life. The second approach (you are bad) marks the child by changing their view of themselves - sometimes for life.

Testimony: When my mother was pregnant with me, her fifth child, her marriage to my father was rocky, and she had discovered in the eighth month of the pregnancy that he was cheating - with her own sister. By the time I was born, she had snapped and had a mental breakdown. Literally, from the time I was born, I was not regarded as important or a priority for my parents and their crumbling world.

I have no memory of being told I was loved or receiving any positivity from my parents. My dad's saying was, *"Better take care of number one because no one else is going to!"* This gave me the message that I was on my own. My parents then split when I was five years old. I have memories of being with my dad sometimes and sometimes with my mom, but we smaller children only have memories of my sister caring for us. She was in her own hell, and I cannot recall her ever being affectionate or loving towards me. Against my father's wishes, I went to see my mother when I was sixteen because I had my own means at this point. When I called him on the phone to go back home his response was, *"Maybe you shouldn't."* His statement had me in tears as I hung up the phone, and my mother asked what was the matter. When she heard what he said, her response was, *"Well, you can't stay here!"*

Not long after this, after I decided I would never speak to my mother again, I gave my life to Jesus. What drew me most was that He loved me so much and that it was unconditional. As touched as I was by His love, I carried my rejection with me into my marriage, into the churches we pastored, and as I went overseas as a missionary's wife. It was so easy for me to tell others that Jesus loved them so much, and, in my heart, I really believed this. But I just could not deeply believe that there was any way God truly loved me.

When Pastor Greg did the series on "Uprooting Rejection," I was blown away that those deeply seated feelings, the beliefs through which I filtered every part of my life, were still there. It was only after going through the entire study that God really set me free, and I can honestly believe that He loves me and accepts me.

Leebon Britoe
I felt so alone & angry

Prayer: As you are continuing on in the book, I now want to pray for some specific issues in the home for God to help you.

God, there are people as they're reading or listening - God, these issues have revealed to them that they have a broken heart. God, You said You bind up the broken hearted. I need You to heal pain in the heart. I'm asking You to do a miracle right now. God, there are parents; they have children - grant them the wisdom, the grace and the love, God, that they would be able with their own children, to show them love and acceptance. God tear down barriers to communication that have arisen in the home. I'm praying You're going to help parents communicate effectively with their children, help children communicate effectively to their parents. Lord God, it is Your will that our homes be blessed, and I am speaking a blessing on their homes. From this moment You're going to begin that process. In the name of Jesus Christ, I thank You for it. Amen.

Greg Mitchell
Chapter 3 – Rejection the Home – Part 2

Chapter 4
Rejection Reactions

John Trent tells a powerful story in the book "The Blessing." He speaks of a man named Brian who was raised by a cold, demanding father. His father was a career Marine officer who tried to instill in Brian the discipline and backbone he felt Brian would need to follow in his footsteps as a Marine officer. Brian had been searching for his father's acceptance and approval all his life, but they always seemed just out of reach. If he scored in sports or did well in class, he would only get a lecture on how he could have done better. He eventually enlisted in the Marines but was dishonorably discharged for attitude problems, disrespect for orders, and fighting. From that point, Brian was no longer welcome in his father's home, and there was no contact between them for years.

Brian began seeking help for some of the unhealthy things he saw in his life. He realized his need for his family's blessing and his responsibility for dealing honestly with his parents.

Then his mother called to say his father was dying of a heart attack. He flew immediately to see his father. During the trip, he hoped they could finally talk and reconcile their relationship. Brian said to himself, *"I'm sure he'll listen to me. I've learned so much. I know things are going to change between us."*

But it was not to be. Brian's father slipped into a coma a few hours before Brian made it to the hospital. The words that Brian longed to hear for the first time—words of love and acceptance—would never be spoken. Four hours after Brian arrived, his father died. *"Dad, please wake up!"* Brian's heartbreaking sobs echoed down the hospital corridor. *"Please say that you love me, please!"* His cries spoke of an incredible sense of loss—not only the physical loss of his father but also the emotional sense of losing any chance of his father's blessing.

The Need For Love

The most basic need in life is love. God created us with an internal hunger for love. We want it so badly because we need it to be emotionally healthy! When we feel loved, it produces emotional health, mental health, spiritual health, and relational health.

- People who feel loved are able to receive and give love.
- People who feel loved are able to process life through the lens of love.

John 13:2-4 NIV ²*The evening meal was being served, and the devil had already prompted Judas Iscariot, son of Simon, to betray Jesus.* ³*Jesus knew that the Father had put all things under his power, and that he had come from God and was returning to God;* ⁴*so he got up from the meal, took off his outer clothing, and wrapped a towel around his waist.*

Jesus was confident in who He was, so He had no problem lowering Himself to the place of a servant.

If the need for love is so built into our hearts, then the Devil tries to ensure that we will be rejected: *Given the message by people that we are not loved and we are not valued.* The lie of rejection (that comes from the outside) produces lies <u>inside</u> of us. You can't receive a message of rejection and stay the same. You can't receive a message of rejection, and it not have an effect on you. It's not like you will hear someone say, *"You are stupid and worthless and I you wish you were never born,"* and you simply reply, *"Okay. So what's for dinner?"*

Reacting Against Rejection

Human nature <u>reacts</u> against rejection – because it's such a violation against our being. People usually either <u>accept</u> the message of rejection as being true – or they <u>fight against</u> the message of rejection being true. Most people's lives are filled with their <u>reactions</u> to rejection. This will play out in:

- Their relationship with God.
- Human relationships.
- Their inner emotional and mental world.

Look at some common reactions to rejection:

Being driven to perform: *People can give us the message that we have no value or that we can't succeed.*
So, some people's reaction against that message is to be driven to win or succeed:

- Driven to make money.
- Driven to succeed in sports.
- Driven to succeed in their career.
- Driven to reach an achievement.

It's not just a desire to achieve – it's a desire to prove our worth to the people who rejected our worth. A desire to prove them wrong. I read of a Mountain climber who had a difficult relationship with his hard-to-please father. He eventually Climbed El Capitan (an extremely difficult vertical rock formation in the Yellowstone National Park) solo. When he reached the top, he started shouting, *"Are you proud of me now, Dad?"* He was yelling at someone who was not even there!

The problem with being driven to perform in order to prove people wrong or prove our worth is that our success or achievements are never satisfying.

- It's never enough: *What's the dollar amount? What is the success measurement?*
- It most likely wouldn't change the opinion of those who rejected us.
- It doesn't really change how we feel about ourselves.

Sadly, some people view the things of God as a means of proving their worth. They exhaust themselves by doing things for God or for the church. They become obsessed with helping people. But it's not actually about God or people-it's about showing their personal value. One man said, *"The dirty little secret about people who are obsessed with saving the world is that they don't like themselves very much."*

CHAPTER 4 — KEY UNDERSTANDING

Some people's reaction against rejection is to be driven to win or succeed.

Seeking counterfeit acceptance: The need for love and acceptance is so strong – we will search for it, even in destructive ways.

- People join gangs or form friendships with unhealthy people: *They're trouble – but they accept me. They want me with them.*

    Judges 11:3 NLT *So Jephthah fled from his brothers and lived in the land of Tob. Soon he had a band of worthless rebels following him.*

- Sexual attention: *Why do some ladies wear sexually revealing clothing?* To gain attention. If men want to look at you, you must be valuable, right?
- Sexuality: Some are driven sexually. They think, *"Somebody wants me – I must be valuable."*

I read the testimony of a Lady who had been very promiscuous for many years. She said, "I hated how I felt after, and I didn't even enjoy the sex, but for a few minutes, I felt loved."

For Men: Sexual conquests can be a constant method of trying to prove manhood or worth.

Single men can be serial fornicators. Married men can be serial adulterers.

- Pornography: The lure of pornography is not just <u>bodies</u>. In some people it is a craving for <u>intimacy</u> - a search for value by making a <u>connection</u>; *but it is a form of false intimacy.*
- Homosexuality: *Homosexuality is a twisting of your identity – where you gain value.*

This can come from sexual violations: I read of a counselor who claimed, *"In 35 years of clinical therapy, I have never met a homosexual whose formative sexual experience was 'normal' – meaning between a boy and a girl."* He said it is always abnormal, involving molestation, incest, pornography, or some other aberration.

This can come from a hard to please or demanding father or mother: They are rebelling against them. This can come from sexual abuse. This can come from your gender being rejected: *Dad wanted a boy, or mom wanted a girl.*

But in homosexuality, the attraction is that *I'm accepted by people like me.* A homosexual can be craving the love they didn't get: *The love of a man or the love of a woman.*

Being Dominated by Rejection

Rejection is an assault on your value or your worth: *It is an assault on your pride – your sense of value.* Our reaction to rejection often is to enthrone pride – to make our pride a god. So, pride now becomes the most important factor in life: *It rules every area of your life.*

Rejection affects your viewpoint – how you see things.

> **Titus 1:15 NKJV** *To the pure all things are pure, but to those who are defiled and unbelieving nothing is pure; but even their mind and conscience are defiled.*

Rejection alters how we see <u>ourselves</u> – how we see <u>others</u> – how we see <u>God.</u> If you were to put on two pairs of dark sunglasses and then look around, you would come to some vision conclusions: *Everything is dim. There must be something wrong with all of you! You're all looking so drab and colorless.* But there is nothing wrong with everyone else – it is your distorted vision. But many people go through life wearing rejection glasses, which makes them see everything incorrectly.

CHAPTER 4 —— KEY ⚷ UNDERSTANDING

Rejection affects your viewpoint – how you see things

Rejected people view <u>everything</u> as a vote on their worth, or as an assault on their worth.

The most common reaction to rejection is interpretation: *Assigning meaning to words or events.* Having believed the lies of rejection, we interpret and assign lies to everything we see.

Look at some of the lies of interpretation:

Rejected people are easily offended: *Every word or action by others is seen as an assault on their worth.*
Think about road rage: We read of people who attack and even kill people over a lane change. The problem is that they are assigning a meaning to the lane change: *They're doing it to disrespect you!*

Angry people are often rejected people: *There is pre-existing, underlying anger because of past rejections.*

> **Genesis 4:23-24 NIV** *Lamech said to his wives, "Adah and Zillah, listen to me; wives of Lamech, hear my words. I have killed a man for wounding me, a young man for injuring me.* 24*If Cain is avenged seven times, then Lamech seventy-seven times."*

- **People get offended by words:** *What did you mean by that?*
- **They get offended by looks:** *Are you looking at me? Are you ignoring me?*
- **They get offended by actions or lack of actions.** When we were pastoring in Johannesburg, South Africa, an older lady in the church who had been attending for quite a while asked me one day, *"Why do you hate me?"* I was stunned! I asked her, *"Why would you think I hate you?"* She said, *"Because You walked past me and didn't shake my hand."* I can have a hundred things going on before any given service that can distract my attention. I shook this lady's hand hundreds of times before that day, but the one time I didn't, she saw that as me hating her or not valuing her.

- **People get offended by events:** Things happen in life; When they are negative, a rejected person interprets the event as a vote on our worth or value. Rejected, insecure Pastors are tormented by the ministry. Everything is personal! A low attendance is seen as an attack when, in fact, it was the flu, the weather, or a major sporting event affecting people.

Rejected people accept false guilt: *They can interpret every adverse event as their fault.* They think, *"I must not measure up – because something didn't work out, or something went wrong."*

They accept guilt for events out of our control, like the weather. Rain washed out the outreach; *I'm a terrible disciple. I'm a terrible a terrible pastor.*

They accept undue responsibility for people: *Other people's salvation. Our children's salvation, or our children's sin.* I've had Pastors call and offer to resign because their adult child has fallen into sin!

The problem with lies is that they produce emotion: *Anger. Hurt. Anxiety. Sadness.* Because we <u>feel</u> things – we assume that means it's <u>true</u>! But we are forgetting that the devil is a liar, and the father of lies!

CHAPTER 4 —— KEY   UNDERSTANDING

Rejected people view everything as a vote on their worth, or as an assault on their worth.

Healing Rejection Reactions

If rejection causes us to enthrone pride, we need to repent of pride. Repent for enthroning our pride.

James 4:10 NKJV *Humble yourselves in the sight of the Lord, and He will lift you up.*

We need to pray, *"God, I recognize this reaction is wrong. I see that not everything in life is about me & my worth!"*

We need healing and deliverance from rejection. We need to ask God for healing and cast out that tormenting spirit!

We need to ask God to enable us to see things clearly and correctly, and not constantly react incorrectly.

Matthew 20:32-34 NKJV *So Jesus stood still and called them, and said, "What do you want Me to do for you?"* [33]*They said to Him, "Lord, that our eyes may be opened."* [34]*So Jesus had compassion and touched their eyes. And immediately their eyes received sight, and they followed Him.*

Testimony: Rejection didn't come from my upbringing; it was a traumatic circumstance that rocked my world and my confidence. It made me question my very identity. I carried shame – not for what I did, but for what other people had done. Through the Sunday School Series, "Uprooting Rejection," the reality that God is my Father, and my identity is in Christ was revolutionary to me! I realized I don't have to live under the cloud of painful events, and I don't have to live in shame. My foundation is Christ, and I can live a fulfilled life.

Her husband adds: The violations that happened to my wife and her family affected her. But the rejection she faced and felt towards herself, and her identity also affected our family, our marriage, and how she helped me conduct our business. It was a spiritual drought that drained the emotional state of my wife and the intimacy God intended. During your roots of rejection

Sunday school, it was amazing for me to see the complete transformation of my wife and witness first-hand the confidence she was able to build in not just her Christian walk - but also her life as a Godly woman, mother and business owner. The uprooting of her rejection has helped her in day-to-day life and built a lasting testimony she has shared in witnessing to several people.

Chris Thorne
Rejected & Started Drugs

Leebon Britoe
Anger Inside

Prayer: Now that you have seen some of the reactions that are produced in you when there are roots of rejection, I want to pray that God is going to begin to help change some of those things in your heart. Let's pray.

God, the people that are reading or listening now, You are revealing to them some unhealthy reactions that they've had toward the rejection that they feel inside. God, there are people that are driven inside in unhealthy ways. God, they need to be set free from that spirit that drives them to achieve or to prove their worth. God, there are people, they have been seeking counterfeit acceptance with unhealthy people in unhealthy ways. They need a deliverance. But God, there are people that they are interpreting. Everything they see is incorrect because rejection is dominating. God, open their eyes, lift those false estimations from off of their mind, let them see clearly. That's what has to happen. Do a miracle. Lord God, open their eyes that they would see clearly in every area of life so that they can find deliverance. And I thank You for what You're going to do in Jesus' name. Amen.

Greg Mitchell
Chapter 4 – Rejection Reaction

Chapter 5
Rejection and Shame

What would they think of me if they knew? She sat in a ladies Bible study looking around at all the other women. She had always somehow felt - dirty. This started when she was a little girl and had been molested numerous times by a family friend. Back then, she somehow thought there must have been something wrong with her for this man to want to do those things to her. In her teen years, she had numerous boyfriends, thinking she would feel differently about herself if she found true love. But somehow, she felt dirtier after each new boyfriend finished with her. She married quickly in her late teens, believing marriage would change everything. But her husband turned out to be abusive and violent. She stayed with him for years because, in a strange way, she somehow felt that she deserved to be treated like that. After she found the courage to leave, a friend invited her to church, and she heard that God loved her. She gladly prayed, turned her life over to God, and was enjoying her new life. But on this day in Bible study, when one of the ladies mentioned the word abortion, her heart began to pound, and she felt almost sick to her stomach. She had an abortion at age fifteen and had tried to blot it out of her memory. When she prayed for God's forgiveness the day she was saved, she initially felt a weight lift off her. But, now, looking around her, a voice in her head said, *"You're not like these other women. They would hate you if they knew what you have done."* She wondered if anyone would be able to guess by looking at her that what she felt deep inside – was shame.

Identifying Shame

We are all social creatures. We live our lives connected to and interacting with other people. Our relationships may include people in our family, our friends, or people at work or school. A sad reality of life is that people can do things that have long-term effects on us.

2 Samuel 13:13 NKJV And I, where could I take my <u>shame</u>?
　　　Tamar is speaking about the effect of her rape by Amnon. She is saying that the impact of this is going to stay with me. I will carry this into all of life.

We need to define shame to identify its work in our hearts and minds.

- *Brené Brown: Shame is the intensely painful feeling or experience of believing that we are flawed and therefore unworthy of love and belonging.*
- *Shame is a vague sense of unworthiness and insecurity.*
　　The message we hear inside is, "I'm not like them. I don't measure up. I don't fit in."
- *Shame is the deep sense that you are unacceptable because of something you did, something done to you, or something associated with you. You feel exposed and humiliated.*

The Roots Of Shame

Shame can come from other people. People can reject us in various ways, and when they do, they give us their opinion of our worth or our identity.

People can produce shame in us through words: *Words have incredible power!*

Proverbs 18:21 NKJV Death and life are in the power of the tongue...

This verse says that death is in the tongue – it has the power to kill. Words spoken can kill our worth. Words can kill faith. Words can kill our identity. When we hear someone say to us words like:

> *You are stupid. You are worthless. What's wrong with you? You are useless.*

Those words can alter things inside of people: They release unhealthy spiritual power.

People can produce shame in us by actions: *Abandonment, divorce, and abuse are three actions that can bring shame.*

The story of Amnon and Tamar is a tragic story of sexual abuse.

2 Samuel 13:14 NLT But Amnon wouldn't listen to her, and since he was stronger than she was, he raped her.

After raping her, he immediately rejects her, which gives the disgusting message: *You are only good for sex.*

People can produce shame in us by failing to give what we need: People who are important in our lives can sometimes fail to give us the things that are vital for our well-being, such as love, affection, communication, finances.

We can open the door to shame through guilt: We have the power of free will. We can choose to do wrong if we want, but when we do wrong, we violate our conscience. Conscience is an inner testimony. When we do wrong, God causes an inner voice to tell us we have done wrong. God allows us to feel bad so we will fix what we have done wrong. Some of our actions would be terribly embarrassing if others knew about them.

Genesis 3:7 NLT At that moment their eyes were opened, and they suddenly felt shame at their nakedness. So they sewed fig leaves together to cover themselves.

The word shame means 'to strip or to be exposed.' *It is a feeling that I am missing something.* This is the root of some addictions. People use alcohol or drugs to make themselves forget, or deaden the pain of guilt. But shame is different than guilt. **Guilt says I have <u>done</u> bad things. Shame says I <u>am</u> bad.**

CHAPTER 5 —— KEY UNDERSTANDING

Guilt says I have <u>done</u> bad things. Shame says I <u>am</u> bad.

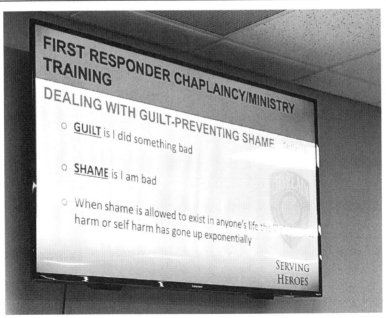

SLIDE SHOWN AT A CHAPLAIN TRAINING COURSE

The Effects of Shame

The story of Tamar in **2 Samuel 13** shows us the deadly effects of shame on the human heart.

You can take on the identity of shame:
Rejection becomes deadly when we <u>internalize</u> the lies of rejection – and <u>make them our own</u>

> *2 Samuel 13:13 NKJV where could I take my shame?*
> *This is <u>my</u> shame – it is a part of me now.*

> *2 Samuel 13:19 she tore her robe of many colors.* She is saying, *"I am different now."*
>> *I <u>was</u> a virgin. I <u>was</u> a princess – but now I have changed.*

> *2 Samuel 13:19 NCV Tamar put ashes on her head...and put her hand on her head. Then she went away, crying loudly.*
>> Ashes on her head: *I'm dirty – here!*
>> She puts her hand on her head: *This is where the problem is!* This is wrong thinking.

Shame is when you agree with someone else's abuse, their hateful words, or their neglect.

A man was walking down the street when he passed a tattoo parlor. He stopped momentarily to look at the various designs you could have inked onto your skin. He saw one design that simply said, "Loser." He was so struck by it he went inside and asked the man behind the counter if people actually got that tattoo. The answer was "Many." The man was incredulous: "Who would willingly tattoo the word 'Loser' on their skin permanently?" The tattoo parlor worker said, "It is written in their heart long before they ever have it written on their skin."

Rejected or abused people sometimes take other people's hateful opinions as their identity. They begin to think: *I am stupid. I am a failure. That's all I'm good for.*

Shame separates us from other people: *2 Samuel 13:19 NKJV ... she went away, crying bitterly...*

- Shame tells us we are unfit to be with other people: *Sometimes, we can't look other people in the eye.*
- Shame separates us relationally: We can isolate ourselves from others – literally! *We keep our distance.*
- Shame separates us emotionally: *They never let anyone get close. Relationships can only stay very superficial.*
- Shame can separate us sexually: *Some people are married, but even in marriage, they still separate themselves because they feel dirty, or they feel unworthy of love.*

Shame causes us to reject ourselves:

- **We tend to re-create our shame with our words:** I have had people tell me the hateful messages they heard from others in the past – but <u>they</u> are now the ones saying it about themselves!
- *I am stupid. I am worthless. I shouldn't be here.*
- **We can tend to harm ourselves:**
  Some people choose self-harm: *Cutting or burning themselves – that's what I deserve!*
  Some people sabotage their own lives, seemingly taking actions that destroy jobs, relationships, marriages, or ministries. *This is what I deserve!*

Tennis pro Andre Agassi was successful by almost any standard, yet his secret meth habit did double duty. It gave him a high and at the same time, "I get an undeniable satisfaction from harming myself and shortening my career. After decades of merely dabbling in masochism (causing pain to myself), I'm making it my mission. I hate tennis, but I hate myself more."

People with shame often pass on shame:

- Victims of shame tend to put that shame on others: *'Hurt people tend to hurt people.'*
  They criticize, mock, or get angry at others for their perceived failures.
- What they hate – they reproduce in others: *It becomes a vicious circle they pass on to others.*
- When we <u>feel</u> shame – we want to <u>put</u> shame on others.

  People who gossip: *Let me tell you how terrible <u>they</u> are!* We make ourselves feel better by telling others about <u>someone else's</u> problems.

  People who blame others: *Genesis 3:12 NCV The man said, "You gave this woman to me and she gave me fruit from the tree, so I ate it."*

  People who use criticism: When you see someone who finds fault with everyone and everything, you see someone who is trying to make everyone look as bad as they feel about themselves.

People with shame assume that <u>God</u> feels about them the way they feel about themselves.

  They're sure God is disgusted with them and that He is turning His eyes away from them.

> *People with shame assume that <u>God</u> feels about them the way they feel about themselves.*

Healing Shame

You do not have to continue to live with shame! Shame is a lie, and God has made provision to heal our shame.

Jesus took our shame to the cross:

Hebrews 12:2 NKJV looking unto Jesus, the author and finisher of our faith, who for the joy that was set before Him endured the cross, despising the shame, and has sat down at the right hand of the throne of God.

Built into Jesus' death on the cross was the element of shame: Jesus was stripped naked and mocked by soldiers, religious Jews, and even the thieves at the cross. He was spit on, paraded through hostile crowds, and executed as a criminal. He bore our shame and became sin for us so He could forgive our sins and change our identity.

Healing shame begins when we see how God views us: The starting point of healing from both rejection and shame is the love of God.

Zephaniah 3:17 NCV "The LORD your God is with you; the mighty One will save you. He will rejoice over you. You will rest in his love; he will sing and be joyful about you."

Knowing everything about us – God <u>delights</u> in us! Like parents singing songs over their babies or young children: You sing because you are glad they belong to you!

We need to <u>believe</u> God's love: *1 John 4:16 NKJV And we have known and <u>believed</u> the love that God has for us. God is love, and he who abides in love abides in God, and God in him.*

Recognize the lies we have believed.
Seek the truth of God's love for us – and believe it!
Look at Jesus: *How He treated people (not the Pharisees). What did He say to people? What did He do for them?* Then we need to personalize it: *That's for me! That's how He will treat me!*

We need to <u>experience</u> God's love: *1 John 4:16 NKJV And we have <u>known</u> and believed the love that God has for us...*

The word <u>know</u> means something experiential/to be certain. In some ways, it means *'to feel.'* We can meet with God!
1. God can bring healing for the past: *Luke 4:18 NKJV He sent me to heal the broken-hearted.*
2. He can bring <u>revelation</u> of His love (that is more than information). *I <u>know</u> – I feel it!*

You may need help in breaking shame: Shame wants us to keep it in. The lie is *"Don't let anyone know."*

Sometimes, when shame comes from someone else, there is freedom in hearing someone else say, *"That's not true,"* or *"What they did was wrong."* I have counseled people who have recounted to me the lies of rejection and shame, and when I tell them, *"those words are lies"* or *"what they did was wrong,"* I have had them tell me later there was a release when they heard that. One person said, ***"It was like a spell was broken off of me."*** I

64

encourage you to seek help from a Pastor or someone who can help you work through these issues.

I end this chapter with one final verse of hope:

Psalm 34:5 NIV *Those who look to him are radiant; their faces are never covered with shame.*

Testimony:
I want to thank God for deliverance! Through the Uprooting Rejection series that Pastor Greg did in Sunday School, so much was revealed that was going on in me that I was oblivious to. I had no idea how much of what I was presently dealing with was something that I could be delivered from. The way I viewed myself, others, and situations was all through a lens of rejection. Words spoken in my past and past violations had embedded in me deep roots of rejection that had detrimentally affected every area of my life. Every hurt and violation watered and fed the perception of not being good enough and many other lies. Words and hurts from my past brought present pain. That pain manifested into anger, which turned into relationship problems and many kinds of issues. I was always on guard and trusted no one. Even around people I considered friends, I always had walls up. I thought brokenness was normal; that I had to feel the pain I've always felt through past violations so that God could use it to help others. I believed a lie that because I was hurt in the past, I had to live broken forever. I didn't realize that I could be set free.

There were times I cried through the whole Sunday School and didn't want to face what was being presented. I felt like everything I could ever be ashamed of was being exposed, and it hurt. Sometimes I didn't even want to go. After some of the Uprooting Rejection lessons, Pastor Greg helped us pray, and I began to feel healing and hope. He also showed us scriptures to help us fight the enemy's lies. So many areas in my heart, mind and soul were impacted and healed. I have a renewed confidence in being a daughter of God!

Chris Thorne
What Am I Doing?

Leebon Britoe
There is no place for me

Greg Mitchell
Chapter 5 – Rejection and Shame

Prayer: Now that you have read or listened to the effect of rejection that has brought shame, I want to pray for you.

God, right now there are people that they are filled with shame - that is a lie from hell. Things have happened to them that have given them the message that there is something wrong with them, that they are bad. That is a lie, and I reject it off of their lives. God, I need You. God, that shame has caused them to separate from other people. It has produced a lack of confidence, both with people and most importantly with You. God, I need You to uproot shame. I rebuke that spirit of shame, that's a lying spirit from hell. God deliver these people, set them free from shame. Cause them to understand how much You love them. And God, they are going to see themselves clearly as You see them, and I thank You for the work that You're going to do. in Jesus' name. Amen.

66

Chapter 6
Rejection and Protection

"I will never again let myself be hurt again." She sat on her bed with her arms clutched around her drawn up knees. Tears rolled down her cheeks as she spoke those words through clenched teeth. She had been dealing with the violent outbursts and abuse from her stepfather for some years now. Little did she know the words she had just spoken to herself would change the course of her life. After she was old enough to leave the house and get on with life, she found that she was suspicious of almost everyone. When someone would try and form a relationship, she would pull away to ensure she couldn't be trapped and abused. She found she had to resort to manipulating other people to try and protect herself. But that only brough other problems. Now some years had gone by, and she realized she was struggling with loneliness and emotional isolation. She thought to herself, *"Is it possible that my plan of protecting myself has simply brought a different kind of prison?"*

Protecting Against Rejection

When we are rejected, this causes emotional pain and feelings that we hate: Feelings of embarrassment and shame, anger, fear, and helplessness. It is completely normal to never want to feel like that again. Only sick people like pain, and intentionally seek or create it in their lives. Healthy people want to avoid pain!

But rejection is the enthronement of pride. Our pride (self-worth) has been damaged in some way, so we react against feelings of worthlessness by enthroning pride. Every decision, every reaction, every aspect of life is determined by pride. Job 41 describes a creature called Leviathan (dragon) Many scholars believe it is a symbolic description of **pride**.

> *Job 41:15-17 NLT The scales on its back are like rows of shields tightly sealed together. ¹⁶They are so close together that no air can get between them. ¹⁷Each scale sticks tight to the next. They interlock and cannot be penetrated.*

This description of the creature of pride shows us: *Pride is marked by defensive armor.* It speak of rows of shields sealed so tightly that nothing can get through. This is a powerful description of many people who have been rejected: Rejected people form **patterns of protection** against being rejected again. You could say rejected people go through life wearing **rejection armor**.

One of the ways we try and protect ourselves from being rejected is by making promises to ourselves. Promises are vows. We usually speak these vows to ourselves in response to pain or shame. We call these **Inner Vows**: Inner Vows are a way to protect our emotions from putting in a place of vulnerability again.

Types of Inner Vows

• **Relational vows:** We may say, *"I'll never trust another person again!" "I'll never get married." "I'll never marry again."*

> *Judges 11:7 NLT But Jephthah said to them, "Aren't you the ones who hated me and drove me from my father's house? Why do you come to me now when you're in trouble?"*

• **Financial vows:** We may say, *"I'll never be poor again!"*

Those who have experienced the stress, moving, conflict or shame of poverty make vows to live in such a way to protect against poverty.

Jimmy Evans tells a story about a man that had cupboards in the house completely filled with sodas. After he got married, he and his wife went grocery shopping together. He began filling multiple carts with sodas. His wife said, *"We don't need that much soda."* He exploded, *"Don't tell me what I can't do!"* He had been raised in poverty. His mom would only let him have water.

- **Failure vows:** *I'll never put myself in that position where I can fail again! I'll never look like a fool again.* Those who feel they failed in the ministry often vow to themselves, *"I will never get involved in ministry again. I will never go out and Pastor a church again."*
- **Marital vows:** After violations in marriage that cause us pain, some spouses vow, *"I won't ever let down my guard again. I will never give myself completely to my spouse again."*
- **Bitterness vows:** People who have been violated, or taken advantage of can vow, *"I'll never forgive them. I'll never speak to them again."* This is not just because we are angry, but because it is protective. We think, *"If I don't forgive, then they don't get another chance to hurt me again."*

Buying Acceptance

There is another form of protection some rejected people take, and that is the protection of buying acceptance. In normal relationships, we do things for other people. But for rejected people, the question is <u>WHY</u>? Do you bless other people because you love them, *or do you do it to get them to love you?*

- Rejected people are eager to help others: *If I do what you want me to do, then you will accept me – you won't reject me. I don't really want to help, but I have to help.*

- Rejected people are eager to give gifts or show attention: Most people show attention by giving calls, texts or visits, and we give gifts when it is appropriate in relationships.

But rejected people do this to buy love or protect against being rejected.

- Rejection blinds us: *We can't see our true motives or sense natural limits in relationships.*

Proverbs 25:17 NCV *Don't go to your neighbor's house too often; too much of you will make him hate you.*

Some people become smotherers: *You move from showing attention to being like a stalker.*

This type of person often resents their 'friend' having relationship with anyone else: *If they have any other friends, then they won't like me!*

The Protection of Control

Rejection often produces feelings of helplessness. We couldn't stop it. We couldn't fix it. So some
rejected people determine to maintain control in life: We think to ourselves, *"If I maintain <u>control</u>, I will never feel helpless again."*

Judges 11:9 NLT *Jephthah said to the elders, "Let me get this straight. If I come with you and if the LORD gives me victory over the Ammonites, will you really make me ruler over all the people?"*

People who have experienced chaos in their lives crave order and control. For one, that manifests in being very comfortable with lots of clearly defined rules in every area of life. For others, they develop obsessive compulsive disorder: *I control things by* *organization.* Some turn to self-harm through cutting: *I can make the pain stop when I want!*

Rejected people often become controlling in relationships. They approach relationships with the attitude, *"You have to go along with my plans, or do things my way - or I'll make you pay!"*

- Some use bribery: They say, *"I'll help you, or I'll give you gifts - but then you owe me."* There's always a price attached to what they give. The result is those we help, or those we give to feel used and violated.
- Some use emotional manipulation: They use anger, tears, outbursts, silence – even sickness; *"You're going to kill your mother. You know how weak your Father's heart is."*

Is it possible that you try and control people so you don't feel the helplessness of rejection?

The definition of manipulation is *Managing or influencing shrewdly or deviously; controlling or tampering for personal gain.*

Galatians 5:19-20 KJV Now the works of the flesh are manifest, which are these; Adultery, fornication, uncleanness, lasciviousness, 20Idolatry, witchcraft, hatred, variance, emulations, wrath, strife, seditions, heresies,

Witchcraft doesn't have to involve sacrificing cats. By definition, witchcraft is *manipulating another person's will. Bending their will to you your own will.*

CHAPTER 6 —— KEY ⚷ UNDERSTANDING

People who have experienced chaos in their lives crave order and control.

Protection Damage

The problem with living by protection is that we are not protected: *We actually do damage!*

- **We damage ourselves:** Words are powerful – they release powerful forces in our lives and hearts.

> *Proverbs 18:21 KJV Death and life are in the power of the tongue: And they that love it shall eat the fruit thereof.*

Our mouths trigger things inside of us: Our entire being lines up with our words, and goes to work to prove our words are correct.

Our emotions line up with our words: *We feel it.*

Our vision is altered: We see things in the way that we spoke.

> *Proverbs 6:2 NKJV You are snared by the words of your mouth; You are taken by the words of your mouth.*

We can become trapped by the spiritual forces we have triggered by our words.

- **We damage relationships:** Relationships function best by openness.

    But when we are protecting ourselves, we are unable to form healthy relationships: *No one can get close to us!*

> *Job 41:15 NLT The scales on its back are like rows of shields tightly sealed together.*

    You wind up offending those you have relationships with. *People don't want to be used, bought, or smothered. They resent being controlled and manipulated.*

- **You block the blessing of God:** God will not make you be free. He will not be force you to be blessed.

Numbers 14:28 NIV So tell them, 'As surely as I live, declares the Lord, I will do to you the very thing I heard you say:

God certainly will not bless manipulation or witchcraft!

Healing From Protection Strategies

There are things we can do to free ourselves from the trap of protections.

- **We need to break the curse of words:**

  Numbers 30:5 NKJV But if her father overrules her on the day that he hears, then none of her vows nor her agreements by which she has bound herself shall stand; and the Lord will release her, because her father overruled her.

Your heavenly Father knows you have spoken words in your pain: *He will release you!*

We need to speak those things out: We need to say, *"I repent! I reject those strategies! I cast out the evil power released by words!"*

Then we need to speak right words: *"I will trust! I will forgive! I will believe! I will try again!"*

- **We need to trust God:**

  Psalm 91:2 NKJV I will say of the Lord, "He is my refuge and my fortress; My God, in Him I will trust."

I don't have to spend life protecting myself: *My Father in Heaven who loves me will protect me!*

- **We need to open up:** Pride wants you to put up walls. *Don't let anyone see the real you. Don't let them know what's really going on. Don't let them in to your heart.*

We need to open up to God: Tell Him, *"I am rejected, afraid, hurting."* He already knows!

Ask God for a miracle of healing & deliverance!

We need to open up to people:

Form relationships with people. Tear down the walls. Let down our guard.

On June 12, 1987, Ronald Reagan stood at the Brandenburg Gate in West Berlin, in front of the famous Berlin Wall dividing East and West Germany. He made a speech that in part laid out his foreign policy approach to Communism. In the middle of the speech, he addressed the General Secretary of the Communist Party in the Soviet Union, Mikhail Gorbachev. He said, *"Behind me stands a wall that encircles the free sectors of this city, part of a vast system of barriers that divides the entire continent of Europe... Standing before the Brandenburg Gate, every man is a German, separated from his fellow men. Every man is a Berliner, forced to look upon a scar... As long as this gate is closed, as long as this scar of a wall is permitted to stand, it is not the German question alone that remains open, but the question of freedom for all mankind. General Secretary Gorbachev, if you seek peace, if you seek prosperity for the Soviet Union and Eastern Europe, if you seek liberalization, come here to this gate.* **Mr. Gorbachev, open this gate! Mr. Gorbachev, tear down this wall!"**

That is God's call to every heart imprisoned by rejection: *Tear down this wall!*

Testimony: When I moved from northern England to the Midlands, I was mocked for having a different accent. When I moved from the UK to Cyprus, I was mocked for being overweight. When I moved to Dubai, I was racially abused and attacked for being British. My parents and I were devastated by the Gulf War, and we lost all we had built up. My peers used and mocked me in many and various childish ways. There was no one big thing. There were just small things all the time.

All of these and more 'attacks' on myself were always unexpected and confused me. I built up a wall of protection from being abused in any way ever again. Whenever I felt under attack, when people tried to speak into my life, I would get angry, shout, fight back, and place that wall between me and them for weeks or months. I would run from things, jobs, people, relationships, church members, and even family. I was always running to 'safety' and away from facing the pain.

By chance, I stumbled upon the "Uprooting Rejection" series on YouTube one day, and it turned out to be a divine encounter that would change my life. From the moment I watched the first episode, I was amazed. I found myself eagerly anticipating each subsequent lesson. I transcribed each video into text painstakingly, creating a written record of the powerful truths that had touched my heart. As I read through these transcripts, it felt like God was speaking directly to me, unveiling layers of pain and insecurity that I hadn't even realized were there. I saw everything through a distorted lens of rejection, misinterpreting communications at nearly every level. Over time, as I immersed myself in these messages, I saw a pattern emerge. I realized that many of my struggles and setbacks were rooted in deep-seated issues of rejection. Whether it was rejection from others, rejection of myself, or even a perceived rejection from God, it had become a barrier preventing me from experiencing the fullness of life Christ promised.

Armed with this newfound understanding, I embarked on a journey of prayer and repentance. I poured out my heart to God, surrendering every hurt, every fear, and every area of my life where rejection had taken hold. And as I did, I felt His healing touch begin to work in me, gradually restoring what had been broken and wounded. It wasn't an overnight transformation, but slowly and surely, I started to see changes in myself. I found myself more confident and more secure in who I was as a child of God. The chains of rejection that had bound me for so long were being broken, replaced by a deep sense of acceptance and belonging in Christ. The key was when I prayed for roots into righteousness, new roots into a new life for me. That prayer changed everything. Today, I can confidently say that the "Uprooting Rejection" series has genuinely transformed my life. Through its simple yet profound teachings, I've been set free from the grip of rejection and empowered to live victoriously in Christ.

Greg Mitchell
Chapter 6 – Rejection and Protection

Prayer: Now that you have finished this chapter about protection, I'm going to pray for you that God is going to help you. God right now, there are people that rejection has caused them to speak words. They have said words and made vows that were not healthy, that have bound them, and affected them in unhealthy ways. God, I break the curse of those words that they've spoken. God, set them free from those words from those inner vows. God, there are people that they have tried to control everything in life to protect themselves from being rejected. God, they've tried to make events be controlled and that hasn't worked. They're trying to control other people and that's not healthy. I need you to do a miracle. Set them free from that spirit of control. God, there are people they have built barriers against others to try to protect themselves. There are married people; They have built walls between themselves and their spouse, and that is killing their communication. It's killing their marriage. God, set them free. Do a miracle. From this moment, Lord God, the barriers of protection that we have erected, God tear them down so they can find freedom in Jesus' name. Amen.

Chapter 7
Rejection, Blame, and a Victim Mentality

"It's not my fault!" the man said angrily. *"You don't know what it was like to be raised the way I was raised!"* He was breathing heavily now, and angry tears formed at the corners of his eyes. The Pastor had requested to speak with him after several angry outbursts with people in the church that included threats of violence. The Pastor asked, *"How many years ago was it since you were treated that way at home?"* The man thought for a moment and said, *"Thirty-two years."* The Pastor asked, *"How long do you intend to allow thirty-two-year-old events to keep ruining your life?*

We all could benefit from having someone in our life asking us that same question.

Blame and a Victim Mentality

Rejection is an assault on a person's worth or value. Being told that we are not loved, not wanted, or not valued causes deep wounds inside us.

> *Psalm 109:22 NKJV For I am poor and needy, And my heart is wounded within me.*

Rejection is not just information; it is a painful, confusing, and tormenting message. Rejected people cannot live with the idea that they are worth less or have no value. It is unnatural to be rejected. You were made to be loved and valued. That is God's plan! So, when we are rejected, we can't just carry it; we must deal with these feelings.

Shifting Blame

One answer is to shift those negative thoughts off ourselves and onto others. We call this **blame**. *The definition of blame is shifting responsibility off us and onto someone else or something else.*

> *Genesis 3:12 NKJV Then the man said, "The woman whom You gave to be with me, she gave me of the tree, and I ate."*

> *Blame explains why we are the way we are: It's someone else's fault!*

Blame is pride enthroned: *I cannot stand to admit I am responsible for any problem.* The reason why it is so difficult to take responsibility in life is larger than any problem you are wrestling with today: *It brings back memories of being shamed or embarrassed.* We equate responsibility with our past shame.

- Blame produces people who never say sorry and never apologize.
  > *Would it kill you to admit that you are wrong or that you did wrong? Would you die if you said sorry?*
- Blame is often aggressive and angry: *It produces explosive reactions of finger-pointing.*

CHAPTER 7 —— KEY ⚷ UNDERSTANDING

Blame explains why we are the way we are: It's someone else's fault!

Human nature tends to extremes: *Shame says everything is my fault. Blame says nothing is my fault.* Reality is balanced: *Some things are not my fault – some things are my fault!*

A Victim Mentality

What goes hand in hand with blame is a <u>victim mentality</u>. A **victim mentality** *refers to a state of mind in which a person feels helpless and as though the world is against them.*

John 5:7 NLT "I can't, sir," the sick man said, "for I have no one to put me into the pool when the water bubbles up. Someone else always gets there ahead of me."

He has an explanation for why he is the way he is, **coupled with helplessness**.

A victim mentality involves <u>self-pity</u>: *Self-pity is a feeling of self-indulgent sorrow over our own sufferings.* In self-pity, we replay past events in our minds that "prove" that we are powerless.

John 5:7 NLT "I can't, sir," the sick man said, "for I have no one to put me into the pool when the water bubbles up. Someone else always gets there ahead of me."

We say to ourselves, *"If only I had better parents, a better spouse, a better job, or more opportunities...then I wouldn't be this way."*

Self-pity produces <u>envy</u>: The man at the pool of Bethesda may have said, *"It's easy for you to talk - you can walk!"* People today may say, *"Of course, you are blessed in life. You had a dad, or you had good parents, or you had a good Pastor."*

Self-pity loves to tell others their pain: The man at the pool of Bethesda speaks out his pain to Jesus: *"I have no one to help me!"* Even though Jesus wasn't asking that!

- **Self-pity can get you attention from other people:** They may say, *"Oh, how terrible. You poor thing! "*

> **1 Kings 21:5 NIV** *His wife Jezebel came in and asked him, "Why are you so sullen? Why won't you eat?"*

- **Self-pity validates our pain:** It makes us think that all our feelings are true and correct, because someone heard our pain.
- **Self-pity gives us a free pass from all responsibility:** *Nothing is our fault if we are victims!*

People with a victim mentality can get strange satisfaction from rejection or things going bad. When bad things happen, it reinforces our victim mindset: *See, they <u>are</u> out to get me! See, it <u>is</u> unfair!*

CHAPTER 7 —— KEY UNDERSTANDING

A victim mentality is an explanation for why we are the way we are, coupled with helplessness.

The Cost of Blame and a Victim Mentality

The danger is that blame and a victim mentality come at a cost.

- **It affects your relationships:** The man at the pool of Bethesda was in a crowd of people, yet he was alone.

When you try so hard not to look foolish, you make yourself look foolish. Other people start to think skeptically, *"It's <u>never</u> your fault?"*

You cause unnecessary friction: People are offended, and relationships never get healed.

> ***Ephesians 4:32 NCV*** *Be kind and loving to each other, and <u>forgive each other</u> just as God forgave you in Christ.*

You wear other people out: People can only listen to so much pain and self-pity before they grow weary of hearing it. Then, they generally start avoiding self-pitying blamers.

Social psychologists Carol Tavris and Elliot Aronson describe how a fixation on our own righteousness can choke the life out of love. They write: The vast majority of couples who drift apart do so slowly, over time, in a snowballing pattern of blame and self-justification. Each partner focuses on what the other one is doing wrong, while justifying his or her own preferences, attitudes, and ways of doing things. ... From our standpoint, therefore, misunderstandings, conflicts, personality differences, and even angry quarrels are not the assassins of love; self-justification is.

- **It blinds you to the possibilities of life:** The man at the pool of Bethesda didn't realize that God in the flesh was standing in front of him. He couldn't see that!

> ***John 5:7 NLT*** *"I can't, sir," the sick man said, "for I have no one to put me into the pool when the water bubbles up. Someone else always gets there ahead of me."*

He responds to God's offer of help with the story: *How bad it's been, how long it's been this way, how unfair it is, how impossible it is to ever change.* The result is bondage to past events and past pain. He has been stuck in life for 38 years!

Steve Maraboli said, *"The victim mindset dilutes the human potential. By not accepting personal responsibility for our circumstances, we greatly reduce our power to change them."*

- **It affects your relationship with God:** You see God as being unfair.

> **Ruth 1:20 NIV** *"Don't call me Naomi (pleasant)," she told them. "Call me Mara (bitter), because the Almighty has made my life very bitter.*

God does not accept our blame and victim mentality.

> **Ezekiel 18:25 NCV** *"But you say, 'What the Lord does isn't fair.' Listen, people of Israel. I am fair. It is what you do that is not fair!"*

Healing Blame and a Victim Mentality

God wants to heal us and set us free from blame and a victim mentality. The story of the man's healing at the Pool of Bethesda is one of only a few miracles that Jesus initiated. The man wasn't asking Jesus for a miracle – Jesus was offering a miracle! The lesson is that God doesn't want us to stay the way we are!

CHAPTER 7 —— KEY UNDERSTANDING

God doesn't want us to stay the way we are!

Look at the path to healing:

You have to decide what you want: *God gives you that power!*

John 5:6 NCV When Jesus saw the man and knew that he had been sick for such a long time, Jesus asked him, "Do you want to be well?"

God will allow you to choose: *I don't want to be bound by fear. I want to have healthy relationships. I want God to use my life.*

The power to choose involves believing God.

Matthew 9:28 NCV After Jesus went inside, the blind men went with him. He asked the men, "Do you believe that I can make you see again?" They answered, "Yes, Lord."

You have to take responsibility:

• Responsibility means we must repent of our pride: *I am wrong sometimes. I am sorry.*

1 Peter 5:6 NIV Humble yourselves, therefore, under God's mighty hand, that he may lift you up in due time.

• Responsibility means we must be honest about our part in our problems in life:

Galatians 6:5 NCV Each person must be responsible for himself.

You may have been rejected and violated in life, but you have to be honest enough to say, *"I share a percentage of my problems. I have also contributed to my own problems."*

• Responsibility means we must break the curse of our words.
Rejected, blaming victims speak things that are the opposite of God's truth. Those words

release a curse: negative spiritual forces into our lives.

> *Proverbs 6:2 NKJV You are snared by the words of your mouth;*

You can pray to God to break the curses of words and claim the blessing of God.

> *1 Chronicles 4:10 NIV Jabez cried out to the God of Israel, "Oh, that you would bless me and enlarge my territory! Let your hand be with me, and keep me from harm so that I will be free from pain." And God granted his request.*

> *Psalm 23:1-6 NKJV ¹The Lord is my shepherd; I shall not want. ²He makes me to lie down in green pastures; He leads me beside the still waters. ³He restores my soul; He leads me in the paths of righteousness For His name's sake. ⁴Yea, though I walk through the valley of the shadow of death, I will fear no evil; For You are with me; Your rod and Your staff, they comfort me. ⁵You prepare a table before me in the presence of my enemies; You anoint my head with oil; My cup runs over. ⁶Surely goodness and mercy shall follow me All the days of my life; And I will dwell in the house of the Lord Forever.*

The Shepherd's Psalm speaks about God's care and provision for us in life. Four beautiful promises that apply to people suffering from the spirit of rejection:

1. He restores my soul.
2. He anoints our heads with oil: He applies healing to our heads – our minds!
3. Goodness and mercy shall follow us in life.
4. We will dwell in the house of the Lord forever: God will always be with us in life and death.

The lame man we read about earlier who was blaming his condition on others decided to take Jesus at his word and do something to find healing.

John 5:8-9 NKJV *[8]Jesus said to him, "Rise, take up your bed and walk." [9]And immediately the man was made well, took up his bed, and walked. And that day was the Sabbath.*

You could make the same choice today, and Jesus would supply miracle power for your healing from rejection, blame and a victim mentality.

Pastor Fred Craddock and his wife were on a short vacation in Gatlinburg, Tennessee. One night, they found a quiet little restaurant where they looked forward to a private meal with just the two of them. While they were waiting for their meal, they noticed a distinguished, white-haired man moving from table to table, visiting guests. Craddock secretly hoped the man wouldn't make it to their table, but he did.

After a short introduction, the white-haired man sat down at the Craddock's table and said, "I've got a story I want to tell you. I was born not far from here, across the mountains. My mother wasn't married when I was born, so I had a hard time. When I started school, my classmates had a name for me, but it wasn't very nice. I used to go off by myself at recess and during lunchtime because the taunts of my playmates cut so deeply. What was worse was going downtown on Saturday afternoon and feeling every eye burning a hole through you. They were all wondering just who my real father was."

"When I was about twelve years old, a new preacher came to our church. I would always go in late and slip out early. But one day, the preacher said the benediction so fast I got caught and had to walk out with the crowd. I could feel every eye in the church on me. Just about when I reached the door, I felt a big hand on my shoulder. I looked up, and the preacher was looking right at me. "'*Who are you, son? Whose boy are you?*' the preacher asked. "I felt the old weight come on me. It was like a big black cloud. Even the preacher was putting me down. But as he looked down at me, studying my face, he began to smile a big smile of recognition. '*Wait a minute,*' he said, '*I know who you are. I see the family resemblance. You are...a son of God!*'" Then he said, '*Now, you go on and claim your inheritance.*' *I left church that day a different person,*" the now elderly man said. "*In fact, that was the beginning of my life.*"

Ben Hooper, former Governor of Tennessee, looked across the table at Fred Craddock and said, "*That was the most important thing anyone ever said to me.*" With that, he smiled, shook the hands of Craddock and his wife, and moved on to another table to greet old friends.

Testimony: My mother and I had a rocky relationship. Being the firstborn, I was naturally under stricter rules. She was doing the best she knew how. However, as I grew up, I had a very insecure view of life. I felt that I could never do enough. I would view things incorrectly through rejection eyes and grievance glasses. I was constantly hard on myself. Although I was in an excellent God-fearing home, I allowed rejection to boil into bitterness. As I grew older, I was 100% interpreting everything as a personal blow or an offense.

When I was eighteen, I had my first genuine conversion experience. I was forgiven, yet I still held the anger from all the wrongs I felt from my relationship with my mother. I cared deeply about how people saw me. I wanted to restore things, but I didn't know how. My pride and bitterness stood in the way.

The fear of rejection stopped the relationship I had always dreamed of.

Then, we were sent out into ministry. I often found myself striving to justify the feelings of pain and bitterness I was living with. This was killing me spiritually. My mind was consumed with this. We would function, but there was constant tension and never a full, loving relationship.

Finally, Pastor Greg called me, and recognizing destructive issues in my heart, he confronted and dealt with me. It was then I finally saw the absolute destruction that my rejection was causing. I began to lay hold of God; I cried out for two days and sought healing. I repented of hatred and bitterness; then I knew what I must do. I contacted my mom. She was shocked; I had basically cut her out of my life. As we spoke, I asked her to forgive me for the way I was treating her; she did likewise, and the healing was beginning.

I remember the most powerful experience was texting the words, 'the resolution I am praying for—like years of hurts and pain erased. ' The instant I hit 'send, ' I broke down weeping. I felt God take my heart of stone and put into me a heart of flesh. Finally, I had the relationship and healing I had always wanted!

Today, this healing has completely changed my relationship with my mom, but also has changed relationships with everyone. I can truly feel the love of God that used to be limited by what I had created in my rejection. My only complaint is that I should have done this sooner. Regardless, I am now walking in freedom.

Prayer: Some of you now by reading or listening God has revealed to you that you have lived using blame or taking on a victim mentality, and you need to be set free. So I'm going to pray for you.

God, right now there are people that they have used blame their whole lives constantly, God, because they are unable to deal with their own rejection. They always have tried to shift responsibility on to other people. That is not working, it's hurting them. There are people that live in self-pity. They have taken on the identity of a victim. They have lost confidence, they have no faith because they view life as being a victim. That is not true. I need You to reach into their hearts. God do a miracle

Greg Mitchell
Chapter 7 – Rejection, Blame and a victim mentality

right now. Allow them to take responsibility in healthy ways. God, let them see they are not victims, but You are able to help them in every situation in life. Do a miracle. As they do take responsibility and choose to believe You, You're going to do a miracle of healing in Jesus' name. Amen.

Chapter 8
Rejection and the Fear of Rejection

"What am I doing here?" she thought to herself. She looked around at the other people at the party. Some of them were already drunk and acting like fools. She hated alcohol. She had seen what it did to her parents, who were alcoholics. As a little girl, she swore she would never drink alcohol. But the good-looking boy in her class who was so popular had been asking her to come to a party for some time. She didn't want to go but hated it when he would tease her, saying, *"What's wrong? Are you too good to party?"* She finally agreed to go but thought to herself, *"I'll go, but I won't drink."* She hadn't been able to sleep for days leading up to the party. She was tormented by the thought of becoming like her parents but even more tormented by the thought of what the other kids in class would think about her if she didn't drink. But when she got to the party, people started offering her drinks. At first, she declined and found something non-alcoholic to drink. But the boy who invited her kept pressing her to have a beer. When he told her, *"Nobody likes boring girls who don't like to have fun,"* she felt sick inside. She could imagine people laughing at her at school on Monday. So, she picked up the beer and began to drink.

The Fear of Rejection

There are two factors inside of us that the enemy uses against us:

Every person has an inbuilt need for acceptance: God made us to gain approval from people

> *Genesis 2:18 NIV The Lord God said, "It is not good for the man to be alone. I will make a helper suitable for him."*
> In a perfect world that would begin with loving parents and continue in life with godly relationships.

Rejected people have negative emotions attached to their events of rejection: The two most common negative emotions that come from rejection are **pain** and **shame**.

> *Psalm 109:22 NIV For I am poor and needy, and my heart is wounded within me.*
> *2 Samuel 13:13 NKJV And I, where could I take my shame?*

So, a spirit of fear is released into our lives: *a fear of rejection.* A rejected person says, *"I don't ever want to feel like that again."* They don't want to feel pain, embarrassment, shame, worthlessness, confusion – or any other negative emotion.

CHAPTER 8 —— KEY UNDERSTANDING

We fear that people will not accept us, and we fear they will reject us.

Because people were involved in our rejection, we often focus our fear of rejection on <u>people</u>. We think, *"I want people to accept me, and I don't want people to reject me."* So, we become afraid of people: **We fear that they will not accept us, and we fear they will reject us.**

Proverbs 29:25 NKJV The fear of man brings a snare, But whoever trusts in the Lord shall be safe.

- The fear of man is a fear of what other people will think of us.
- The fear of man is a fear of what other people will say to us or do to us.
- The fear of man is a fear of what other people will <u>not</u> say to us or do for us.

The fear of man, or fear of rejection causes us to want to please people. **We try and please people to keep them from rejecting us.**

CHAPTER 8 ——— KEY UNDERSTANDING

We try and please people to keep them from rejecting us.

Fear of rejection can manifest in many ways:

• Fear of rejection can cause us to violate our conscience.

> *John 19:12-13 NIV From then on Pilate sought to release Him, but the Jews cried out, saying, "If you let this Man go, you are not Caesar's friend. Whoever makes himself a king speaks against Caesar." [13]When Pilate therefore heard that saying, he brought Jesus out and sat down in the judgment seat in a place that is called The Pavement, but in Hebrew, Gabbatha.*

• Fear of rejection can cause us to make wrong decisions or sin.

1 Samuel 15:24 NKJV Then Saul said to Samuel, "I have sinned, for I have transgressed the commandment of the Lord and your words, because I feared the people and obeyed their voice."

Fear of rejection causes people to smoke, drink, take drugs, have sex with other people, steal, commit crimes – and commit any other sin or wrong action. The people who did these things often didn't actually want to do them, but fear of rejection caused internal pressure to do them.

- **Fear of rejection can cause us to deny God.**

Matthew 10:33 NKJV But whoever denies Me before men, him I will also deny before My Father who is in heaven.

- **Fear of rejection can cause us to be unable to be honest.**

People with problems or needs will not ask for help because they are tormented by the thought, *"What will they think of me?"*

Sometimes people lie about their sin or cover up their sin. Their reasoning is, *"I didn't want to disappoint you."*

- **Fear of rejection can cause us to be unable to say no.**

We will all meet people who want us to do what they want. Sometimes, we don't want to, but fear of rejection keeps us from saying no. We get requests for help or requests for money. We don't have the time and can't afford the money, but we can't say no. Rejected people find it hard to say no to salespeople, so they buy things they don't want and cannot afford.

The Damage of The Fear of Rejection

The Bible says the fear of rejection is a <u>trap.</u>

     Proverbs 29:25 NKJV The fear of man brings a snare, But whoever trusts in the Lord shall be safe.

- The one trapped has their life determined by the one who trapped them.
- The trapped one is stuck: *They make no progress in life.*

Look at some of the damage done by the fear of rejection:

- **We are often unhappy:** We do things we don't want to do, which produces resentment inside.
- **We can be guilty:** We become guilty because we know we're doing wrong. By doing what other people want, we are violating God's word and our conscience.

     For people with a fear of rejection, serving God and going to church is a torment: *We don't fit in with unsaved people, and we don't feel right with saved people!*

- **We can struggle in relationships & have relationship problems:**

We feel manipulated and used by the people we can't say no to.
  - We start resenting them.
  - We start avoiding them: *We avoid them because we can't be honest about our feelings.*

- **We can get involved in sin and doing wrong:**

We wind up doing damage to ourselves and our relationship with God.

Matthew 10:33 NKJV But whoever denies Me before men, him I will also deny before My Father who is in heaven.

Man-pleasing is **idolatry**: You are worshipping someone's opinion more than Almighty God!

Exodus 20:3 NKJV "You shall have no other gods before Me."

We can lose our souls.

Matthew 10:28 NKJV And do not fear those who kill the body but cannot kill the soul. But rather fear Him who is able to destroy both soul and body in hell.

Edward Welch said, *"What is the result of...people-idolatry? As in all idolatry, the idol we choose to worship soon owns us. The object we fear overcomes us. Although insignificant in itself, the idol becomes huge and rules us. It tells us how to think, what to feel, and how to act. It tells us what to wear, it tells us to laugh at the dirty joke, and it tells us to be frightened to death that we might have to get up in front of a group and say something. The whole strategy backfires. We never expect that using people to meet our desires leaves us enslaved to them."*

Healing The Fear of Rejection

To be spiritually and emotionally healthy, we need to get free from the trap of man-pleasing: the fear of rejection.

We need to be healed of the wounds of rejection.

Luke 4:18 NKJV "The Spirit of the Lord is upon Me, Because He has anointed Me To preach the gospel to the poor; He has sent Me to heal the brokenhearted, To proclaim liberty to the captives And recovery of sight to the blind, To set at liberty those who are oppressed;"

Notice in this scripture that healing comes <u>before</u> liberty. Healing <u>produces</u> liberty.

We need to repent of idolatry: If we have made <u>people</u> idols, we must repent.

> *Genesis 35:2 NKJV And Jacob said to his household and to all who were with him, "Put away the foreign gods that are among you, purify yourselves, and change your garments."*

We need to trust God.

> *Proverbs 29:25 NKJV The fear of man brings a snare, But whoever trusts in the Lord shall be safe.*

We must trust God's opinion of our worth.
We must trust that our life and future is in God's hands.

> *Daniel 3:17-18 NKJV If that is the case, our God whom we serve is able to deliver us from the burning fiery furnace, and He will deliver us from your hand, O king. 18But if not, let it be known to you, O king, that we do not serve your gods, nor will we worship the gold image which you have set up."*

The Work of God
Choosing to get free from pleasing Man is what causes God to work on our behalf.

> *Proverbs 29:25 NKJV The fear of man brings a snare, But whoever trusts in the Lord shall be safe.*

Safe: That means we will be protected from sin, and protected from bad decisions.

Matthew 10:32-33 NKJV *"Therefore whoever confesses Me before men, him I will also confess before My Father who is in heaven.* *33But whoever denies Me before men, him I will also deny before My Father who is in heaven."*

Daniel 3:24-25 NKJV *Then King Nebuchadnezzar was astonished; and he rose in haste and spoke, saying to his counselors, "Did we not cast three men bound into the midst of the fire?" They answered and said to the king, "True, O king." 25"Look!" he answered, "I see four men loose, walking in the midst of the fire; and they are not hurt, and the form of the fourth is like the Son of God."*

God worked powerfully for those who did not allow man-pleasing and fear of rejection to compromise their faith. No doubt, He will be the fourth man in fire in our lives. You are not alone in life's trials.

Testimony: Growing up I was rejected physically, mentally, emotionally and spiritually. Raised in a very religious home filled with a lot of demonic realms. I grew up viewing everyone through a lens of betrayal, disappointment and hurt. I didn't trust anyone - especially men. I grew up hating my parents and viewed people of authority as people who only let you down.

I gave my life to Jesus at age eighteen and once I saw people around me disappoint me. I had family leave the Church. There were ungodly relationships that didn't work out. Even though Jesus had done a great miracle in my heart and life, I still held on to rejection. I would hear sermons and feel so convicted, but I didn't know how to change it. As the years rolled on, I lost many relationships and friendships. I saw that people around me didn't want to be around me for one reason or another. I always thought it was them; they had the problem, not me. I viewed myself as the victim.

We had become Pastors and had been out for a few years when Pastor Greg started the rejection series. I started to watch them with great intentions of being open to change and wanting a miracle from God. I thought God had helped me, until a few years later we had become missionaries and on the mission field things are magnified so much more. I began to fall into old habits, mind sets and attitudes. For years I had family issues, I didn't trust my Pastor, and had a hard time seeing God's love for me.

It came to a breaking point where I had to be confronted about my attitudes and actions. I was about to lose it all if God didn't do a miracle. I watched Pastor Greg's rejection series once again and read a book about rejection this time. I cried out to God, asking for a miracle in me. A miracle in my heart, my mind, and my life. I asked for forgiveness from those who I had hurt, and from God himself. God did just that.

He has done such a miracle in my life. He has restored my relationships; especially with a family member that has been broken for over twenty-four years. We are close now, we talk on the phone almost daily, and we even say we love each other. God has moved in my relationship with my pastor. He helped me to see how much I am loved and cared for. I now see God's love through a whole different lens. I can now process things in life through Gods lens instead of a lens of rejection. He has corrected my spiritual lens and now I can receive things from him and others as they were intended.

I know where my acceptance come from. I am a daughter of the King and I'm so very thankful for his faithfulness and love. Thank you, Pastor Greg, for your faithfulness and for obeying God in his word and dealing with issues that needed to be dealt with.

Life is still going to be hard and have its ups and downs, but God has renewed my heart and appreciation. I see life so differently now and can see the curse of rejection that has been broken off my life and my family. I had built a wall straight up to heaven and wondered why I wasn't getting breakthroughs. Now the wall has been demolished and the oil can flow.

Rejection is such a demonic stronghold; I am so very thankful I am delivered.

Greg Mitchell
Chapter 8 - Rejection and the Fear of Rejection

Prayer: Now that you've read or listened to this chapter, you have seen that the fear of rejection is the work of hell that has been produced in your life, and I want to pray for you.

God, there are people that, because of the wounds of the past, they have been afraid of being rejected again. It's affected them in every area of their life. Some of them are dominated by a fear of what other people would think of them. It's made them make decisions that are not based on Your will, but based on fear, to ensure that they never be rejected again. That is a work from Hell and I reject it. God set them free from that fear. I cast it out of their lives. The fear of man, God, we repent. We have made people idols and that is wrong. We repent, and I'm asking that You're going to cause people now to see things clearly. That fear will no longer dominate them. You're going to do a work of deliverance. Instead of fear, give them confidence, power, love, and a sound mind. That's their portion. And I thank You for what You're going to do. In Jesus' name. Amen.

Chapter 9
Rejection and Marriage

"Where did our love go?" he asked, with tears running down his cheeks. He looked at the smashed pieces of the plate she had thrown at him and the hole in the wall he had punched in frustration. He thought, *"We used to be so in love, but now it seems like all we do is spend our time going round and round in circles, fighting about everything. Fighting about nothing."* He couldn't even remember how this fight started. He thought he made a comment that she somehow was offended by, and she said hateful words she would later regret. In the middle of the fight, she screamed at him, *"You're just like my dad!"* and he yelled his response, *"And you're just like my mom!"* Those were not good comparisons for either of them, but they suspected it might be true. They both knew they couldn't keep going on like this, but the sad part is that neither of them had any idea of how to change.

In 2 Samuel, we see a real-life example of how rejection works in marriage. Rejected people usually bring their rejection issues into marriage.

2 Samuel 6:16, 20-23 NIV ¹⁶*As the ark of the Lord was entering the City of David, Michal daughter of Saul watched from a window. And when she saw King David leaping and dancing before the Lord, she despised him in her heart.* *2 Samuel 6:20-23 NIV* ²⁰*When David returned home to bless his household, Michal daughter of Saul came out to meet him and said, "How the king of Israel has distinguished himself today, disrobing in the sight of the slave girls of his servants as any vulgar fellow would!"* ²¹*David said to Michal, "It was before the Lord, who chose me rather than your father or anyone from his house when he appointed me ruler over the Lord's people Israel—I will celebrate before the Lord. 22I will become even more undignified than this, and I will be humiliated in my own eyes. But by these slave girls you spoke of, I will be held in honor." 23And Michal daughter of Saul had no children to the day of her death.*

Rejection Baggage

To understand the importance of the marriage story of David and his wife Michal, we need to see the background of this woman Michal. Her story is a life filled with rejection.

- **She was used by her father:** He saw no value in her, except as a <u>tool</u> for his own purposes. He
offers her to David as a kind of winner's trophy. Then, later on, he tried to use her to get her own husband killed.
- **Her father rejected her because she helped her husband:** When she did not help her father capture her husband, but instead helps David escape – her father gave her away to another man. This was to spite David. Once again, she was a tool to be used against her father's enemies.
- **Then she was forced to compete with six other women for David's attention**: No doubt that would damage your self-esteem: *I'm not good enough for my husband...*

But their story shows a universal problem with many marriages: **We bring our rejection issues into marriage!**

CHAPTER 9 —— KEY   UNDERSTANDING
We bring our rejection issues into marriage!

Rejection is an opinion of value: *Someone gives the message that another person has no value or less value.*

- We can hear <u>general</u> rejection messages that are directed at many people: This could be statements such as, *"All men are pigs"* or, *"Never trust a woman."*
- Or we can hear specific rejection messages aimed at us personally: This could be statements such as *"You are stupid,"* *"You are worthless,"* or *"Your sister or brother is much better than you."*

Michal had these messages directed at her: She learned from her father that, *"Men are pigs and can't be trusted. Men will use you."* From her husband, she got the message, *"I am not good enough."*

The important point is that rejection alters how you view things in life.

> *2 Samuel 6:16 NIV As the ark of the Lord was entering the City of David, Michal daughter of Saul watched from a window. And when she saw King David leaping and dancing before the Lord, she despised him in her heart.*

For men: *Rejection alters their view of women.* For women: *Their view of men - can be formed by rejection.*

CHAPTER 9 —— KEY UNDERSTANDING

Rejection alters how you view things in life.

Some people have a spirit of fear put into them by watching their parents' dysfunctional marriage.

When children see the conflict, pain, and chaos of their parent's marriage, a natural reaction against that is to put up <u>walls</u> to protect ourselves. We don't want conflict, pain, and chaos!

•

- Some people's wall of protection is to say, *"I will never get married."*
- For others' their walls go up in their marriage. They say, *"I will make sure you never hurt me or make me feel like I did growing up."*

We view our spouse through the lens of how we view ourselves.

God made you to have value and worth. This is supposed to come first and primarily from your relationship with Him.

> ***Mark 12:31 NCV*** *The second command is this: 'Love your neighbor <u>as you love yourself</u>.'*

This scripture shows us an essential point in relationships: If you don't love yourself (in a healthy way) or don't think you have value or worth, you won't be able to handle it when someone loves you more than you love yourself. I have counseled people who have severe rejection issues in their lives. When their spouse says, *"I love you,"* you would think their reaction would be: *"That's wonderful! Praise God!"* Instead, they respond with a mystified, *"Why?"*

People with unhealed rejection issues try to <u>sabotage</u> their love relationships. The easiest way to do that is to pick a fight with your spouse:

> ***2 Samuel 6:20 NLT*** *When David returned home to bless his own family, Michal, the daughter of Saul, came out to meet him.*

She said in disgust, "How distinguished the king of Israel looked today, shamelessly exposing himself to the servant girls like any vulgar person might do!"

Rejected people don't have reasonable conversations about issues that bother them. They fight and attack our worth; *"You're stupid, you're no-good, you're ugly, you're useless."*

In a strange way, we try to recreate the rejection we experienced at home! People push or attack their spouses until they are rejected by them *because it matches how they feel about themselves!*

Rejection twists communication.
We often <u>speak</u> from a place of hurt: The old saying, *"Hurt people – hurt people."*

2 Samuel 6:20 NLT When David returned home to bless his own family, Michal, the daughter of Saul, came out to meet him. She said in disgust, "How distinguished the king of Israel looked today, shamelessly exposing himself to the servant girls like any vulgar person might do!"

Conversely, we also <u>hear</u> from a place of hurt: *Rejected people filter and interpret what they hear through their rejection.*

- Women hear their husbands say, *"You look beautiful."* But their reaction is, *"You don't really mean that. You just have to say that."*
- Men can hear their wives speak about almost any issue: *"You didn't pay a bill,"* or *"You forgot to take out the trash."* But their reaction is, *"So you think I'm stupid?"*

The result is that couples <u>fail</u> to communicate because of hurt: They don't know how to communicate or are afraid to.

Bitterness poisons relationships:

Hebrews 12:15 NLT *Watch out that no poisonous root of bitterness grows up to trouble you, corrupting many.*

When we have been hurt or violated by other people's rejection, a common reaction is to hold on to anger and violations toward those who rejected us. We usually bring our bitterness into each new relationship. And just like Hebrews says, it corrupts, damages, or ruins the relationship.

Think about this: **You may not actually be fighting with the one you're fighting with right now!**

Couples have a fight, and one spouse says, *"That's just like my dad! You're just like my ex-wife or my ex-husband! "*

Rejection Damage
Look at how rejection affects your marriage:

Rejection affects your viewpoint:
You see things in a twisted way. Michal saw her husband rejoicing, but her reaction was, *"You made a fool of yourself and acted like a pervert!"*

Titus 1:15 NKJV *...but unto them that are defiled and unbelieving is nothing pure; but even their mind and conscience is defiled.*

Rejected husbands or wives can't enjoy what is good or what their spouse is doing right; they can only see what's bad and what they are doing wrong.

When counseling marriages, I sometimes ask each spouse, *"Can you tell me something good about your spouse?"* Unfortunately, I have had some spouses say, *"Nothing!"* My response is, *"Wow! Then sadly, if you keep seeing things like that, you won't stay married."*

Rejection affects your viewpoint.

Rejection can kill love:

The tragedy of Michal is love that died.

> *1 Samuel 18:20 NLT ...Saul's daughter Michal had fallen in love with David*

But then her rejection issues caused her to attack and tear down her love for him.·

> *Proverbs 14:1 NIV The wise woman builds her house, but with her own hands the foolish one tears hers down.*

When people say, *"We're not in love anymore,"* that *doesn't just happen!* Couples fall out of love when they attack each other and re-create the pain from the past. They fall out of love when they fail to give the needed love. They fall out of love when they strangle their love to death.

Rejection blocks blessing: In the story we read, David was going to bless his household. Everyone in the house should have received the benefits. But Michal stopped the blessing at the door, and *David didn't force his way in!* The lesson from that is that **you can't be blessed _and_ bitter!**

> *Matthew 18:35 NCV "That's what my heavenly Father will do to you if you refuse to forgive your brothers and sisters from your heart."*

The blessing the King wanted to give the servant, He would not give - because of the servant's unforgiveness.

Bitterness cuts us off from God's love and favor. That's why some prayers go unanswered—because bitterness causes blockage!

Mark 11:24-25 NIV *"Therefore I tell you, whatever you ask for in prayer, believe that you have received it, and it will be yours. 25And when you stand praying, if you hold anything against anyone, forgive him, so that your Father in heaven may forgive you your sins."*

Rejection affects our fruit: *2 Samuel 6:23 NIV* *And Michal daughter of Saul had no children to the day of her death.*

- Our spiritual fruitfulness can be blocked: *This is speaking about our ability to win souls.*
- We can also hurt our physical fruitfulness: *This means we can do damage to our children.*

Choosing A Different Ending

Sadly, there was no happy ending for Michal: She was never healed of her bitterness. The Bible says in *2 Samuel 6:23 NIV And Michal daughter of Saul had no children to the day of her death.*

But David is a contrast to his wife Michal: *David was also rejected and violated in life!*

- His own father despised David: When Samuel told David's father to gather his sons for a special ceremony, his father didn't even bring David because he didn't see potential in him.

- He was falsely accused by his brother.
- King Saul was ungrateful to David after he risked his life to help.
- He was slandered, plotted against, and attacked by Saul. Saul separated him from his wife, and his wife was given to another man.

This is what's amazing to me in life: I see people who experienced the same past circumstances, but they wind up with completely different hearts and totally different outcomes. One person is made bitter, twisted, and emotionally imprisoned, while another is made better. In fact, their past becomes the basis of future blessings!

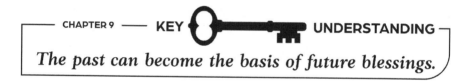

CHAPTER 9 ——— KEY   UNDERSTANDING

The past can become the basis of future blessings.

David made different choices than Michal:

He brought the violations of life to God:

David wrote many of the Psalms, which are filled with honest prayers. He would tell God, *"You see what's happening. You see what people are doing to me. I don't know if I can make it!"*

You must deal with rejection and the violations of life through forgiveness:

I choose to let it go and leave it with God. *"God, I need your help dealing with how I feel about what's happened to me."*

Job 42:10 NIV *After Job had prayed for his friends, the Lord made him prosperous again and gave him twice as much as he had before.*

David found his true value in God:

> *Psalm 8:4-5 NIV* *4what is man that you are mindful of him, the son of man that you care for him? 5You made him a little lower than the heavenly beings and crowned him with glory and honor.*
>
> *Psalm 139:14 NCV* *I praise you because you made me in an amazing and wonderful way. What you have done is wonderful. I know this very well.*

David sought to be a blessing to others:

> *2 Samuel 6:18-20 NCV* *18When David finished offering the whole burnt offerings and the fellowship offerings, he blessed the people in the name of the Lord All-Powerful. 19David gave a loaf of bread, a cake of dates, and a cake of raisins to every Israelite, both men and women. Then all the people went home. 20David went back to bless the people in his home...*

Giving out to bless others when you are hurting is a crucial discipline that will enable you to survive violations in life.

Make the choice to bless others - especially your spouse.

Testimony: Two weeks after we got married, my husband's parents got a divorce. At the same time he told me of his parent's divorce, he told me he should have never married me. My husband rejected me, just like his father rejected him. He spoke about it as if it happened yesterday.

My husband cheated on me repeatedly, with no regard for God or our marriage. I had to deal with a broken heart, work through anger, and wrestle with bitterness. I told God my husband must choose to make our marriage work. My husband did make a choice. He wanted to go.

Rejection wanted to entangle me in my personality, mind, and heart, so I would respond with a deep fear, just like it did in my husband. After two decades of rejection as an unloved wife, my actions flowed from my rejection. I wanted to have worth, to matter, to have value. I tried to find where I could be useful. I got hyper-involved in every ministry I could in the church. Pride took the place of rejection. I was creating my worth, my value, and why I mattered. I didn't put my family first but instead placed ladies' church functions first. Later, when my kids were older, they complained about my priorities. I was performing; Working for the Kingdom of God, but with misplaced motives and priorities.

My choices in money were rooted in rejection. I bought things for myself and my children to make me feel good, and my uncontrolled spending became an obsession.

I thank God he is patient and faithful. He revealed my heart to me slowly over time. When Pastor Greg taught the "Uprooting Rejection" series, I responded to God's love and leading. It was like going through a file of each destructive mentality and behavior. I was so done with living with rejection. I wanted to be free. I didn't run from the hurt and pain of the rejection because I knew Jesus loved me, and I wasn't alone in coping with the ugly truth. God showed His truth for my deliverance. I prayed, *"God loves me. Rejection is not my portion. It is a lie from hell, and the Blood of Jesus will break its power. I will trust God and do His Will."* God wanted me to be healed more than I did.

When God showed me His love, I received healing and deliverance. God has changed my heart. I am different in so many ways. I am free.

Greg Mitchell

Prayer: You now have seen that rejection affects marriage in profound ways. I'm going to pray that God is going to begin to help you.

God, there are people right now in their marriage rejection is doing damage. God, some of them have brought their baggage from the past into this relationship, and it's hurting them. God, they are interpreting. They are seeing their spouse in ways that are not accurate because of rejection; That their viewpoint is distorted. That communication has been damaged in their marriage. They're not able to speak clearly. They're not able to hear correctly, and that's hurting them. God bring healing into these marriages. As I'm asking You, set them free. Let them see clearly. Let them hear clearly. Heal them and allow them to get rid of anything from the past that is bringing damage in the present. God, I speak blessing over every marriage of the people who are reading or listening. Do a miracle. God, bless their relationship. And then let it flow from their marriage into everyone that they come in contact with. In Jesus' name. Amen.

Chapter 10
Rejection and Money

"It feels like you're cheating on me," he said through gritted teeth, *"with a credit card!"* *"You secretly applied for a new credit card without telling me,"* he waved his arm at the packages piled up on the table, *"to buy more stuff? Are you deliberately trying to ruin our finances?"* Her voice rose, and tears sprang to her eyes as she shot back at him, *"It feels like you don't love me! All this stuff,"* she waved her arms at the packages, *"makes me feel beautiful. Would you prefer that I feel ugly and unhappy? What good does it do if our finances are perfectly in order – but we are miserable?"*

Money And Emotions

It's important to understand that money is not just math. Money is not just needs and bills.
Money is emotional! *Money is closely connected to your emotions.*

- **We make money choices based on how we feel inside:** Pre-existing emotions at work influence what we do with our money.
- **Money makes us feel certain ways:** Money produces feelings. Spending money produces certain feelings, and not spending money makes us feel certain ways. Having surplus money produces feelings, and not having enough money produces feelings.

So, **rejection affects our emotions:** Rejection isn't just information. When someone tells us we are stupid or worthless, we don't just say, *"Oh, OK. Thanks for sharing that."* Rejection causes pain, confusion, hopelessness, and anger. *We can carry these emotions under the surface.*

Your emotions affect your viewpoint: *You <u>see</u> things based on your <u>feelings</u>.*

In this case, **Emotions affect how you view money!** Some basic questions about money we need to answer in our own lives:

- What is the purpose of money?
- How is money to be used?

>   *Proverbs 11:24-26 NKJV There is one who scatters, yet increases more; And there is one who withholds more than is right, But it leads to poverty. 25The generous soul will be made rich, And he who waters will also be watered himself. 26The people will curse him who withholds grain, But blessing will be on the head of him who sells it.*

CHAPTER 10 —— KEY UNDERSTANDING

Emotions affect how you view money!

Rejection and withholding.

For some people, money is connected to fear.

- **Some people grew up in poverty:** For them, money was the cause of constant turmoil. There was a constant fear that they might not be able to eat. They never knew when they might suddenly have to move, or things might be repossessed.
- **Some people grew up with conflict over money:** They saw their parents constantly fighting over money. Money conflicts

- produced terrible feelings. Money conflicts caused threats of divorce.

This produces an obsession with security: People will often say repeatedly, *"I have to take care of the future!"* This desire for security isn't based on wisdom, but <u>fear</u>: *"I don't ever want to feel like I did when I was young again!"*

> *Exodus 32:23-24 NCV The people said to me, 'Moses led us out of Egypt, but we don't know what has happened to him. Make us gods who will lead us.' ²⁴So I told the people, 'Take off your gold jewelry.' When they gave me the gold, I threw it into the fire and out came this calf!"*

God's people wanted the security of something they could see. Notice that it was a god, and the god was made of gold! Gold was supposed to provide security.

- **The person obsessed with security may struggle to tithe:** They may struggle to start tithing, or they start, but then they stop: *A bill came!* They fear that <u>God</u> will put them in a position that will make them feel like they did in the past.
- **The person obsessed with security may struggle to obey God and give:** Their fear is, *"What if I don't have enough later?"*

  If they don't break that fear off their life, they will miss God's blessing and may never get ahead financially.
- **The person obsessed with security hates to spend:** *I won't have enough!*

> *Proverbs 11:24 NKJV there is one who withholds more than is right, But it leads to poverty.*

If money is causing conflict with those you love, there is a problem.

I'm not talking about conflicts caused by surprise spending without consultation: *You bought a boat without discussing it?*

I'm talking about when you try to discuss the possibility or need to buy or spend: *But it turns into a war!*

If money is causing intense emotional reactions with those you love, there is a problem.

It's possible to make everyone in the family suffer because you are afraid to spend any money.

- **An extreme version of fear about money manifests in hoarding:** People hold on to unnecessary junk – but they don't think it's junk!

They insist, "I can't let go of this stuff. What if I need it later? I could sell it! This is good stuff!"

If the thought of getting rid of things is causing an emotional reaction: *Something's wrong!*

If the thought of getting rid of things is causing conflict with your family: *Something's wrong!*

In 2013, A 76-year-old Canadian man had to be rescued by firefighters after spending at least two days trapped under piles of junk inside his cluttered home. Police had received a report about a man that had not been seen or heard from for several days. When they responded, they found the doorway and halls of the man's home blocked with mounds of rubbish. They found the man with an injury to his leg, which had been pinned under debris, cutting off circulation for several days. It is possible that the man may lose his limb because of the incident, officials said. The man had a lucky escape: Officials say had they not received a report about the elderly hoarder who was found dehydrated and suffering from circulation problems, he likely would have died.

Rejection and Spending

Some people are the opposite: They view money as a way to <u>fix</u> their negative emotions. To this person, money <u>produces</u> emotions; *It makes them feel certain ways.*

- **Some use money as a <u>drug</u>:** It provides a way to escape their problems.

  They think, "I'm sad or stressed – so I'm going shopping. My problems go away with the thrill of buying." Shopping has the same effect as alcohol or drugs – and is every bit as addictive!

- **Some use money as <u>medicine</u>:** They are trying to heal a negative emotion inside.

  Rejection is an assault on one's worth or value. So, people buy things to try to produce a feeling of value.

  If they wear designer labels, own designer bags, wear designer shoes: They somehow think they are worth more because they have better clothes, bags, or shoes!

  They think if they buy a car of worth, they become worth more!

  What you wear, drive, or own – DOES NOT change what you are inside!

  This kind of thinking usually produces debt: *They will <u>overspend</u> to try and buy worth!*

Some use money as a competition: The old saying, *"Keeping up with the Jones's."*

A false idea is that if I have more than you or something better than you, I then have more worth than you!

When we pastored in Johannesburg, South Africa, we lived in a housing complex: twenty-seven homes behind a common wall. Because we all lived in the complex together, you could see other people's houses. However, I noticed after moving in that my neighbors treated possessions like a competition: If one person bought a BMW, soon a neighbor would buy a BMW convertible. If one person installed a pool, another would install a pool with a fancy slide. I purchased a basic single-axle trailer to haul equipment for the church. Shortly after, my neighbor bought a double-axle trailer with a fancy paint job.

Money and a Poverty Mentality

Rejection is an opinion about our worth or value that we get from other people. Sometimes, people have received the message that they are no good or worthless. Their rejection of our worth becomes incredibly destructive when we <u>accept</u> the opinion of others and <u>agree</u> with it.

This plays out in how some rejected people view money:

- **The guilt syndrome:** People have been told they don't deserve anything, or that they'll never amount to anything. But then they get some money, and can buy decent things, or succeed in their job or business. Their blessings cause inner turmoil because the voice in their head says, *"I shouldn't have this! I don't deserve this!"*

   ***Proverbs 10:22 NKJV** The blessing of the Lord makes one rich, And He adds no sorrow with it.*

   The blessings of God shouldn't make you feel sorrow, but rejected people sometimes don't enjoy blessings – they feel guilty about them. Sometimes they feel compelled to give things away: They think, *"I shouldn't have this."* In extreme cases, they may even deliberately sabotage their blessings.

117

- **The poverty syndrome:** People who have accepted rejection feel they have no worth or less worth, so their financial situation will match their opinion of themselves.

Everything they have is cheap, low-class, broken, worn out junk: *The quality or the condition of what they own matches their opinion of their worth.*

If you give someone with a poverty mentality something nice: *They will soon trash it to match their mindset – their view of themselves.*

CHAPTER 10 —— KEY   UNDERSTANDING

People who have accepted rejection feel they have no worth or less worth, so their financial situation will match their opinion of themselves.

A Healthy View of Money

We need to see the road to financial health:

Be healed of whatever pain that is affecting your viewpoint.

Form a correct view of your worth and value: An accurate view of our worth comes when we understand <u>God's</u> opinion of our value! (We will look at this in depth in later chapters.)

Begin to see money correctly:

- **Money is a tool:** Money is given to us by God so we can use it to help in life. We can use money to help with the things of God, to help ourselves and to help other people.

Proverbs 11:25-26 NKJV The generous soul will be made rich, And he who waters will also be watered himself. 26The people will curse him who withholds grain, But blessing will be on the head of him who sells it.

- **God does not mind His children being blessed financially:**

    Genesis 13:2 NKJV Abram was very rich in livestock, in silver, and in gold.

    Philippians 4:12 NCV I know how to live when I am poor, and I know how to live when I have plenty. I have learned the secret of being happy at any time in everything that happens, when I have enough to eat and when I go hungry, when I have more than I need and when I do not have enough.

    Romans 8:32 NKJV He who did not spare His own Son, but delivered Him up for us all, how shall He not with Him also freely give us all things?

- **The key to financial health and prosperity is generous releasing of money.**

    Proverbs 11:24-25 NKJV There is one who scatters, yet increases more...25The generous soul will be made rich, And he who waters will also be watered himself.

We release to God through tithing and giving offerings.

We should also release finances by giving to other people in need.

A key Biblical revelation is that we can have our needs met and have money <u>without it causing misery</u>.

⚷

We can have our needs met and have money without it causing misery

Testimony: Husband: My parents were Pastors and raised me well, but we moved every few years. I never felt like I belonged because most other kids had grown up together, so I never felt accepted. I felt like I had to earn people's praise. I would try and imitate everyone else to fit in. I felt like my life was under a microscope or magnifying glass in church. The ushers and Sunday school teachers held me to a higher standard than any other kids, and I tried to live up to it, but it was never enough. So, I became a people pleaser for fear of being rejected. After salvation, I tried to please everyone around me and earn their love and acceptance.

Wife: I felt rejected by my dad from a very early age because he and my mom were never together. He was constantly in and out of my childhood. He would promise to come pick us up over the weekend. We would get dressed and wait by the window for him all day from 8:00 am to 10:00 pm, but he would never show up. Once it hit 8:00 pm, I knew he probably wasn't coming, but I would still wait. I would cry silently. I didn't want my grandma to see me crying since she would be mad at us for staying at the window, knowing he wouldn't show up. This scarred me as I grew up. I viewed everyone through the lens of rejection. My relationship with my parents, friends, Pastors, and especially with God was filtered through the lens of rejection.

Because of our spirit of rejection, we felt like we didn't deserve more in life, or to be blessed. Therefore, we accepted poverty and lived with it. If everyone else rejected us, then maybe that's how God viewed us, too. Why should we expect Him to bless us?

- We didn't feel we deserved a nice car, so we lived with a broken, ugly one because it was good enough.
- We thought we didn't deserve a nice house, so we lived way below our means and wouldn't buy a house.
- Whenever a blessing came to us, we felt bad about it.
- When I would get a raise, we felt bad about it.
- If we saved up and bought a nice car, we felt bad about it.
- We usually never had savings because we would give all our money to God. Not necessarily out of love, but almost trying to buy God's love and acceptance. So, if something broke, we had no money to fix it. So, things would stay broken.

I broke free from rejection by recognizing that we were constantly dealing with the fear of rejection and had become people pleasers. During the "Uprooting Rejection" series, I realized how many areas rejection affected me, and I wanted to be free. So, I began praying about it and asking God to heal me. I wrote out a list of scriptures that I began to claim about who I was in Christ, and I prayed over them. One day, my wife asked me about a conversation I had with Pastor Greg. She asked, *"What did you tell him, and how did you say it?"* I got fed up with *the thought of being so careful about what I said, so I said, "I don't care what he thinks about me. If he thinks I'm an idiot, let him deal with me. If he thinks I'm proud, let him tell me so. At least he'll know where I'm at and will be able to help me and guide me."* Both of us realized that I was definitely on the road to healing from rejection.

My wife broke free from rejection when she came for counseling, and Pastor Greg helped her recognize that she had rejection issues that stemmed from her childhood. He prayed for her and gave her a book on rejection. It went from head knowledge to her heart. She began claiming the scriptures mentioned in that book about who she was in Jesus; finding her identity in Him and not in performance or people's opinions.

Whenever she felt thoughts of rejection, she began to rebuke it in prayer and fight against it.

We both recognized that we had a spirit of poverty when Pastor Greg preached a sermon at a conference addressing it. We identified ourselves and began to make changes in our lives. We immediately started saving money and fixing things when they broke. We bought nicer vehicles, cleaned them regularly, and fixed them when they needed to be fixed. For the first time, we bought a house. Then I started a business, and God blessed us with financial increase! Last year, we made more than I have ever made in my life in one year.

Leebon Britoe
Effects of Poverty

When we understood our value in Christ, our view of money changed, and the spirit of poverty was broken off our lives.

Greg Mitchell
Chapter 10 - Rejection and Money

Prayer: You have now seen how rejection affects your view of money. So, I'm going to pray that God is going to help you in this area.

God, rejection distorts our viewpoint of money. You know that. So, I'm asking You help every person that that's true in their life. Some of them God, they were raised with poverty and it has dominated. It's produced fear. It's producing an obsession with money and that is not healthy. God, there are people they use spending as medicine. They use money in unhealthy ways. God, bring healing to their heart so that they see You correctly - they're able to see money correctly. Therefore, they're able to make right decisions in the area of money. I speak blessing on every person in their finances as they honor You and gain a correct understanding of what money is for, and how to use it. Bring blessing into their lives. In Jesus' name. Amen.

Chapter 11
Rejection and Rebellion

"How dare he!" he thought, as he watched the Pastor preach. He sat seething inside with indignation while the sermon was going on. The Pastor had spoken to him before church about a conflict with someone in the church. The man had offended him, so he lost his temper and started yelling at him in the church hallway. He may have even said a bad word or two. But the Pastor dared to tell him that his actions were unacceptable in church and inappropriate as a Christian! He didn't even care that the other guy had looked at him and laughed! *"I think he's just biased against me. I bet he likes the other guy more than me, so he took his side,"* he thought angrily. *"He's just like my Dad. That's what he used to do with me when I was young. He always told me I was wrong and couldn't treat my brothers that way."* He decided, *"I'm not going to put up with it. I bet there are many other people who don't like the way the Pastor treats them. I'll ask around. Besides, his sermons haven't really done much for me lately. I just don't feel the presence of God here anymore."*

That scenario plays out in many different ways in churches worldwide. People who have been rejected in the past are in danger of allowing rejection to become rebellion against authority.

The Roots of Rebellion

Every person has authority figures in their life. These people are supposed to provide wisdom and direction. They give instructions and commands to achieve that. Our authority figures can be parents, teachers, bosses, coaches, or Pastors.

In a perfect world, they would use their authority in a healthy way to benefit you. They would try to help you. They would speak to you with love, wisdom, and balance.

Unfortunately, for many people, this is not what happens. The most common source of rejection is an authority figure, such as a parent, teacher, boss, coach, or Pastor.

When rejection comes from an authority figure, some people's reaction is **rebellion**.

CHAPTER 11 —— KEY UNDERSTANDING

When rejection comes from an authority figure, some people's reaction is rebellion.

The Essence of Rebellion

Rebellion is a rejection of authority. The word 'rebellion' suggests hostility against authority. It usually involves disobedience: *I won't do what you say.* Some people seem to live their whole lives with their fists up, ready to fight.

> *Genesis 16:12 NLT* "*This son of yours will be a wild man, as untamed as a wild donkey! He will raise his fist against everyone, and everyone will be against him. Yes, he will live in open hostility against all his relatives.*"

Rebellion is a viewpoint: It's a way of looking at authority. Those whom people in authority have rejected go through life trying to protect themselves against being rejected by anyone else in authority. So, rebellion usually manifests as an attitude of <u>suspicion</u> and <u>fear</u>.

Rebellious people are suspicious of anyone in authority. Even if there has never been a violation by the current person in authority, they are certain they can't be trusted.

Rebellious people are afraid of anyone in authority. They are convinced that anyone in their life who has authority or any form of leadership is not safe. Rebels are afraid that the person in authority will embarrass you, hurt you somehow, or abandon you.

Rejection brings <u>past</u> pain into <u>present</u> relationships: The tragedy of rebellion is that it's not a level playing field. The person in authority is at a disadvantage in the relationship because they are not just dealing with their own words or actions but fighting against past violations and rejections that had nothing to do with them! The spirit of rejection tells the rejected person lies! It's a lie that every person in authority is just like the person who rejected and violated you in the past. It's a lie that anyone in authority is out to get you or cannot be trusted. Sometimes, as a Pastor, I get intense reactions from people that are not in line with the issue I am trying to deal with in that moment. When that happens, I realize, *"They're not simply fighting with me – they are actually fighting with someone from their past!"*

CHAPTER 11 —— KEY 🔑 UNDERSTANDING

Rejection brings <u>past</u> pain into <u>present</u> relationships.

---

3 manifestations of rebellion

Separation from authority: The reaction of some rejected people is to stay away from the person in authority in their lives. Some people may attend a church for years, but they never ask a question, ask for advice, and never open up about what's going on inside. Some people literally never get near the Pastor at all. The twisted reasoning of rejection is, *"If I never get near you, you can't hurt me, you can't embarrass me, and you can't destroy my life."*

Rejecting authority: There will be instructions in any human relationship involving a person in authority. This may be in the family (parents), in class (teachers), on the job (bosses), or in the church (Pastors). All of these people in authority must give advice, instructions, or correction from time to time. This may help equip you personally or help the group of people function correctly without problems.

But rebels reject advice, instructions, or correction. They may even fight against it!

> *1 Samuel 15:13-14 NLT When Samuel finally found him, Saul greeted him cheerfully. "May the Lord bless you," he said. "I have carried out the Lord's command!" 14"Then what is all the bleating of sheep and goats and the lowing of cattle I hear?" Samuel demanded.*

The root of rebellion is pride: I know better! Pride can be based on perceived success that inflates our sense of worth. Past rejection can produce a reaction that fights fiercely to defend our sense of worth. Either way, it's just pride.

We see this in a rebel's reaction to instructions.

- Rebels want to do something other than what someone in authority tells them.
- Rebels can get upset when someone in authority tells them what to do.

Some people are open rebels: They get angry and shout. They bow their necks and glare defiantly at the person in authority.

Some people are quiet rebels: They are like King Saul in the scripture listed above. They smile cheerfully as though they agree with you and will comply, but then they go ahead and do what they want to do. They do what they think is best.

Attacking authority: Rebels are driven to find <u>flaws</u> in those in authority.

2 Samuel 15:2-3 NKJV Now Absalom would rise early and stand beside the way to the gate. So it was, whenever anyone who had a lawsuit came to the king for a decision, that Absalom would call to him and say, "What city are you from?" And he would say, "Your servant is from such and such a tribe of Israel." 3Then Absalom would say to him, "Look, your case is good and right; but there is no deputy of the king to hear you."

Rebels will scrutinize every word and action of someone in authority to find fault. If they find a fault or a flaw, in their minds, it 'proves' why those in authority can't be trusted. They think a flaw 'proves' why they should be independent and reject all authority.

Rebels usually enlist others. Rebels will never be rebels alone. Like Absalom, they first find something they disagree with, don't understand, or are upset at in the one who is in authority. Then, they emphasize it to enflame other people. They say, *"That is so unfair! I can't believe they did that to you!"* I sometimes get people who come to me and say, *"A lot of people are saying..."* I stop them and say, *"You mean <u>you</u> are saying – to some people you talk to."* When rebels find others who are upset and seem to agree with them, they think it 'proves' why they should be independent and reject all authority.

In the history of our Fellowship (Christian Fellowship Ministries), almost all the rebellious Pastors who have left our Fellowship and done damage have had rejection issues. This was often rooted in their own troubled relationship with their fathers or the fact that they never had a father. Their rejection caused them to view their own Pastor with suspicion and resentment, which ultimately opened the door to rebellion in their hearts.

The Cost of Rebellion

The great danger of rebellion is that it separates you from healthy relationships. Being a loner is unhealthy. You become the sole authority on every issue of your life! If that is how you operate in life, you will come to the wrong conclusions because you're not seeing things correctly.

>*Proverbs 12:15 NKJV* *The way of a fool is right in his own eyes: But he that heeds counsel is wise.*

- **Rebellion causes you to lose the benefit of wisdom.**
As a Pastor, I see people in the church struggling. I see Pastors struggling. I know I could help them, but they will not ask for help. They will not ask for advice. They will not listen to advice that has been given. Rejection has produced rebellion, and rebellion will not receive direction from anyone in authority.

- **Rebellion causes us to miss the blessing of God.**

God is the one who designed life to operate on the principle of authority! He has determined that every person needs to have someone in authority over them to help them, not hurt them! But people get upset at the person in authority in their life, so they reject authority. They say, *"I'm rejecting a person,"* but, in some way, they are actually rejecting <u>God's</u> authority! I get calls from people in congregations complaining about their Pastor. Sometimes, there are legitimate issues that I can help them to resolve – if they want to! But in extreme cases, I have told people, *"You think you have a Pastor so-and-so problem (fill in the name yourself), but you actually have an <u>authority</u> problem!"* If we reject God's plan of authority (which is called rebellion), God will not bless our rebellion.

- **Rebellion brings destruction:** The stories in the Bible about rebellion are stories of destruction – because rebellion brings destruction!

1 Samuel 15:23 NKJV *For rebellion is as the sin of witchcraft, And stubbornness is as iniquity and idolatry. Because you have rejected the word of the Lord, He also has rejected you from being king."*

Witchcraft is supernaturally blinding: Rebels are blinded. I have seen rebellious people make the most foolish, destructive decisions. But these decisions make sense to them!

In the Bible, we see that God <u>fights</u> rebellion! I challenge you to look at the word <u>rebellion</u> in the Bible and see how often it refers to God <u>judging</u> rebellion. One reason God judges rebellion is that it is destructive to others. I could spend hours recounting the stories of damage and destruction that rebellion brought: Destruction to children, marriages, ministries, callings, and entire churches. I could tell you stories of the turmoil and division in relationships that rebellion caused. Worst of all, there are people in hell today because of rebellion: People that backslid over the turmoil they saw in the church or people who never heard the Gospel because a church's mission was destroyed by rebellious people. Sadly, the people who caused this destruction often had the roots of rebellion formed by rejection.

Healing Rebellion

God has designed life to work with authority.

> **Romans 13:1 NKJV** *Let every soul be subject to the governing authorities. For there is no authority except from God, and the authorities that exist are appointed by God.*

If God is the one who designed authority and places people in authority, the fact that you were rejected or violated by someone in authority in the past does not give you the right to reject authority! What needs to happen is that we need to be healed from the rebellion rejection has produced in us.

- **We need to forgive those in authority who have violated or rejected us.**

> **Colossians 3:13 NCV** *Bear with each other and forgive whatever grievances you may have against one another. Forgive as the Lord forgave you.*

It doesn't make sense to let the past ruin the present or your future! Take your pain to God and ask him to heal you. Tell God, *"I forgive those people."* To forgive means to release or let go of the violation. It is simply telling God, *"I am not the judge. I leave those people with you."*

- **We need to repent of our pride and humble ourselves:** We are not the world experts on everything in life. We are not the sole authority of what is correct in life, nor do we determine the way everything in life should operate!

    1 Peter 5:5 NKJV Likewise you younger people, submit yourselves to your elders. Yes, all of you be submissive to one another, and be clothed with humility, for "God resists the proud, But gives grace to the humble."

- **We need to accept Godly authority in our lives:'**
    - We need to seek Godly authority: Ask for advice or help.
    - Flow with authority: Go along with the direction that is being given. Don't resist and fight every decision being made.
    - Work with flawed authority: Every person in authority has flaws – but that does not mean they are evil! That doesn't mean that everything they say or do should be rejected. We must have a correct attitude about working with someone in authority when we see their flaws. The Bible tells of Noah getting drunk and how his sons dealt with his mistake. One son (Ham) went and told his brothers: He wanted to expose his Father's mistake to others (and perhaps rejoice over it). But the other 2 brothers approached it differently:

    Genesis 9:23 NLT Then Shem and Japheth took a robe, held it over their shoulders, and backed into the tent to cover their father. As they did this, they looked the other way so they would not see him naked.

They were not saying what their father did was acceptable, but they were saying, *"We need to deal with this problem – while still respecting his position of authority in the family."*

God was pleased with this attitude, for when Noah spoke, he released a Divine blessing on Shem and Japheth:

Genesis 9:26-27 NLT *26Then Noah said, "May the Lord, the God of Shem, be blessed, and may Canaan be his servant! 27May God expand the territory of Japheth! May Japheth share the prosperity of Shem, and may Canaan be his servant."*

That is the choice every person must make when dealing with rejection from those in authority, as there is the potential for rejection to become rebellion.

Leebon Britoe
No rules... Freedom

Greg Mitchell
Chapter 11 – Rejection and Rebellion

Prayer: You now see that rejection has affected some of you in the area of rebellion. You need a miracle, and I'm going to ask God to heal your heart.

God, there are people right now, they have been hurt and rejected by people in authority. That has affected their entire viewpoint of authority. They are suspicious of authority. They resent authority. They resist authority in every area of their life. The Devil has lied to them about godly authority now. Rebellion has been produced in their heart. They need a miracle. God, they cannot survive rebellion. I'm asking You to set them free. I cast out rebellion. I cast out suspicion. I cast out the fear of authority. From this moment, cause them to begin to see authority correctly. Let them draw close, let them seek godly authority. Let them flow with the decisions of authority. God's anointing flows from the head down, and now let the oil flow in their lives as they respond correctly in deliverance from rebellion. In Jesus' name. Amen.

Chapter 12
Rejection and a
Performance Mentality

The man was angry. *"I didn't like what you said in your sermon tonight!"* The Pastor asked, *"What part?" The part where you said that people who fail or backslide can be redeemed."* The Pastor was dumbfounded. *"Then what should happen to them?"* he asked. The man angrily said, *"They should be done away with! They don't deserve to be redeemed!"* The problem was that sometime later <u>that</u> man failed and fell into sin. But he could not get over it and was never seen again.

Sadly, that is a true story. Knowing people, that man no doubt had deep rejection issues. He viewed his relationship with God as being based on his personal performance. And if he ever failed to perform well, he couldn't survive.

That is an illustration of how rejection can produce a performance mentality in serving God.

The Roots of Performance

Rejection plants roots deep into our hearts and minds, and these roots produce all sorts of unhealthy fruit. Two kinds of rejection produce deadly roots:

The first is rejection rooted in performance:
Some people experienced conditional love or acceptance from parents or others. All love and acceptance came with

a huge **IF**. They were given the message: *"I will love and accept you only if you do what I want, do what is right, and act like your sibling. You will be loved and accepted only if you win, succeed, or get good grades."*

Genesis 27:4 NCV When you prepare the tasty food that I love, bring it to me, and I will eat. Then I'll bless you before I die

- **Some people found that they could never do enough.** They tried to do the things they were told would bring love and acceptance, only to find there were further expectations: *Do more! Do better!* So their feeling of love and acceptance was always <u>uncertain</u>: *Am I doing enough to be loved? Am I good enough to be accepted?*

- **Some people lived the roller-coaster of love and acceptance.** Their parents would tell them, *"I love you today,"* but then tomorrow they would be told, *"I'm disgusted with you."* So, any love or acceptance always brought uncertainty, because it would never last.

- **Some people discovered the basic truth about themselves:** *At times, you will <u>not</u> measure up!* You won't win sometimes. You won't succeed in everything. You're not like someone else. You won't be good, and at times you will do wrong. What then? So, it produces hopelessness: *I'm never going to be loved and accepted because I can't measure up.*

The second is rejection rooted in guilt or Shame: *Other people can give us the message of Shame.* Shame can begin with guilt over things we have actually done wrong, but then other people remind us of what we've done. They hold it over our heads. They cut us off in disgust. They tell us, *"How could you do something like that?"*

136

I met a man who told me this story about his father. *When he was a little boy, he was running in the house, being naughty. His pregnant mother chased him, and while chasing him, she slipped and fell. As a result of the fall, she wound up losing the baby. So, the family banished him. They sent him away to live somewhere else.* His family were some kind of Christians. He told me the story to explain why his father never went to church when he grew up.

For others, the rejection they experienced was simply their family's opinion of shame. They attached deadly messages when you didn't measure up. **The message was not that you've <u>done</u> wrong - but that you ARE wrong!** Perhaps someone said, *"There's something wrong with you!"*

This produces a deadly effect when we accept their false opinions as true. Brené Brown explains, *"Shame is the intensely painful feeling or experience of believing that we are flawed and therefore unworthy of love and belonging."*

The Effect of Rejection After Salvation

Think about what happens when a performance-based person becomes a Christian and enters a relationship with God. By the time they get saved, some people have already spent a lifetime trying to perform, striving to gain love and approval from people. Then they hear about God's love. *"God can be your Heavenly Father!"* That is supposed to be good news.

Unfortunately, they now view the relationship between God and themselves through the eyes of the past.

- For some, the news that God is your Father is not good news at all! Their only experience with a Father was <u>all</u> negative: *That means that God will hurt them, abuse them, abandon them, and can't be trusted.*

-

- For others, their view is that God will be demanding, hard to please, and fickle and that He will change His mind about His love for them.

— CHAPTER 12 —— KEY   UNDERSTANDING

We can view the relationship between God and ourselves through the eyes of the past.

The Performance Mentality

So, what rejection often produces is a **performance mentality** in serving God:

- **The first wrong approach: I will make up for the past – I will make up for my shortcomings.**

Matthew 18:26 NCV "But the servant fell on his knees and begged, 'Be patient with me, and I will pay you everything I owe.'

    Christians with this mentality do what is right - not because of love or because it's right: *But to pay God back and make up for their sins or failings.*

    Luke 15:19 NIV I am no longer worthy to be called your son: make me as one of thy hired servants.

- **The second wrong approach: I will earn or deserve God's love.**

It is a mistake to think you can clean up your own life. That is the mistake of false religion: *I've done enough to be good enough!* Have you ever heard someone say, *"If my good deeds outweigh my bad, I will go to Heaven?"*

But some born-again Christians have similar faulty reasoning. They are doing right things to try and <u>make</u> God love them. They read their Bibles, pray, come to church, give money, and witness to others, but under the surface, they are wondering about God: *"Do you love me now?"*

Some work for God in the hopes of earning His love and favor. They help in the church, are involved in multiple ministries every night of the week - *not <u>because</u> of love, or because it is right, but to <u>earn</u> God's love!*

- **The third wrong approach: If rejection came through people, I can gain God's approval through people.**

This kind of person focuses their efforts in serving God on pleasing and impressing people!

Matthew 6:1-2 NIV "Be careful not to do your 'acts of righteousness' before men, to be seen by them. If you do, you will have no reward from your Father in heaven. ²"So when you give to the needy, do not announce it with trumpets, as the hypocrites do in the synagogues and on the streets, to be honored by men. I tell you the truth, they have received their reward in full.

Matthew 6:5 NIV "And when you pray, do not be like the hypocrites, for they love to pray standing in the synagogues and on the street corners to be seen by men. I tell you the truth, they have received their reward in full."

This text speaks of those who seek God's validation of love & approval – through people!

The Damage of Performance

Performance-based Christianity is exhausting: The nature of works-based religion is that it adds burdens in life.

> **Matthew 23:4 NIV** *They tie up heavy loads and put them on men's shoulders...*

This gives the message of *"Salvation is the blood of Jesus AND...clean up your act or work hard and try to be perfect."*
- Working for God's love is exhausting!
- Trying to gain approval from people is exhausting!

Guilt is the mark of a performance mentality. Sometimes people do what is right simply because of guilt. I've known people that were imbalanced. Witnessing to unsaved people is good, but they feel constant guilt. They can't drive down the street or go grocery shopping without being constantly distracted by the urge to witness. *"I have to stop the car. I can't just buy lettuce at the store and go home. I have to witness to every person – this could be their last chance!"* They are not doing it because of love but because of guilt.

Performance-based Christianity is uncertain: In a performance relationship, your value, worth, and identity are based on what you do and how well you do it. But there's a problem: *How do you know if you've done enough? Says who?* So, performance-based Christians are tormented: *Could I have done more? What if someone else says I'm not doing enough?*

1 John 3:20 NKJV For <u>if our heart condemns us</u>, God is greater than our heart, and knows all things.

This produces a life filled with pressure: *What happens if you have a bad day? What happens if you sleep in or you're sick, so you miss prayer, outreach, or church?* This person doesn't do right because *"I get to"* or *"I want to"* but *"I must. I HAVE TO!"*

CHAPTER 12 —— KEY ⎯⎯ UNDERSTANDING

Performance-based Christians are tormented.

God does not bless performance-based Christianity: When you approach God with an attitude of, *"I want to work for and earn Your love and approval,"* You are saying something about <u>Him</u>, not you! You are telling God, *"You're not loving. You're hard to please. You're hard to get along with."*

Matthew 25:24-25 NCV "Then the servant who had been given one bag of gold came to the master and said, 'Master, I knew that you were a hard man. You harvest things you did not plant. You gather crops where you did not sow any seed. 25So I was afraid and went and hid your money in the ground. Here is your bag of gold.'

Performance-based Christians are saying, *"What Jesus did on the cross is not enough!"*

Galatians 3:3 NIV Are you so foolish? Having begun in the Spirit, are you now being made perfect by the flesh?

The result of these errors is that you never enter into God's rest.

Hebrews 4:3 NLT For only we who believe can enter his rest. As for the others, God said, "In my anger I took an oath: 'They will never enter my place of rest,' " even though this rest has been ready since he made the world.

Rest means peace and confidence in God's love. It means we can stop the works of performance to try and gain God's love and acceptance.

Performance-based Christians do not experience the supernatural favor of God: *That attitude and approach displeases Him.*

CHAPTER 12 —— KEY UNDERSTANDING

Performance-based Christians do not experience the supernatural favor of God.

Freedom From Performance

Look at the path to freedom from performance-based Christianity:

We must recognize the truth: We CANNOT pay God back. We cannot make up for the past!

Matthew 18:24 NLT In the process, one of his debtors was brought in who owed him millions of dollars.
It would be the equivalent of owing hundreds of millions of dollars. If you make $15 an hour, you can never pay it back!! But our sin is much more expensive than money: It required the blood of a perfect man - God in the flesh. We can never, ever pay God back for our sin.

We must repent of our pride and unbelief:

It is prideful to think we can be good enough and pay God off! Our puny human efforts are laughable when we think of God's perfection.

It is unbelief when we will not accept God's love for us and the payment he already made!

We must accept God's love: Relationship with God only works if you accept <u>His</u> terms. God's terms of relationship are based on love!

Matthew 18:27 NLT Then his master was filled with pity for him, and he released him and forgave his debt.

It had nothing to do with the servant and everything to do with the master!

- Our sin is already paid for! You <u>cannot</u> make any other payments!

1 John 1:9 NKJV If we confess our sins, He is faithful and just to forgive us our sins and to cleanse us from all unrighteousness.

- Your Heavenly Father ALREADY loves you. You don't have to try and make Him love you. I love my grandchildren very much! They don't have to work hard to earn or deserve my love. They already have it! How much more is that true of God's love for us?

1 John 3:1 NIV How great is the love the Father has lavished on us, that we should be called children of God! And that is what we are! The reason the world does not know us is that it did not know him.

Testimony: I was raised in a great home with a loving father and a stay-at-home mom. Life was fairly normal, but I suffered from a lack of self-esteem. I always felt like my worth was based on my performance. If I didn't get straight A's, my parents told me to work on it. I was driven (within myself) to be a perfect child, but I never felt like I was quite good enough. Maybe that was because I was conceived illegitimately, or maybe because my mother's parents divorced when she was young and she passed it on to me.

Whatever the reason, I always felt I needed to prove that I was worth something. I carried that quest for perfection into adulthood and salvation. I was always striving to be the best, stand out, and be worthwhile. I had to be involved in everything and couldn't rest unless I was the best. Even compliments from others didn't help my torment because I never believed them anyway. I hadn't proved to myself that I was worth something. That was never going to happen.

I got a lot of feedback over the years from my husband, my pastor, and others that I needed to relax and that I was too pushy. I would think, *"Relax, are you crazy?"* Pastor preached one time that if you're an A-type personality, maybe God doesn't want you to do anything! I was thinking, *"What does that even mean?"* The idea of doing nothing was pure torture to my soul. I could not relax without getting depressed. My poor husband must have felt so inadequate; I couldn't even enjoy a meal out with him without breaking down and crying. I couldn't enjoy myself unless I was doing something.

During a Bible conference a few years ago, I finally realized something needed to change. Besides helping with the conference, we were overbooked, trying to get together with as many people as possible and having people over every day &

every night. I was exhausted. I was driving myself into the ground! I decided this had to stop. God had begun to work on me through Pastor Greg's series on uprooting rejection.

For the following conference, I only scheduled two things. As I was driving home, I was so relieved that I could just go home & rest. I thought, *"Wow, this is different! God has done something!"* I can enjoy being home now & doing nothing occasionally. I can enjoy hanging out with my husband again. I can laugh again, even at myself! That is a miracle! I don't have to be perfect! I am loved by the God who made me. I am loved just like I am. I don't have to accomplish anything to prove I'm worthy of His love. I can just be me, and it's ok. What a glorious relief! Years ago, my pastor gave me a book, Free Yourself, Be Yourself. Well, Finally, I can say I'm free to be me!

Thank you, Jesus, for making me & loving me. And dying for me so I don't have to kill myself trying to prove I am somebody!

Leebon Britoe
I prayed for the first time

Greg Mitchell
Chapter 12 – Rejection and a Performance

Prayer: You now have seen how rejection produces a performance mentality in your heart, so I want to pray for you.

God, there are people. They have relationship with You right now, but rejection has distorted what that relationship should be like. God, some of them, they do not have confidence in Your love. So, they are trying to earn Your love when they already have it. God, I cast out that that spirit that causes them to think they have to perform. I rebuke fear. When they do not have confidence in Your love, that fear is going to leave. God, open their eyes. Let them see how much You love them. God, there are people that they have fought in the church and with other Christians. They have to have their approval, and that will make them be loved. That's a lie. Set them free from that lie. Let them rest in Your love. And it is not dependent on their performance. God, You are gracious to us. You are a God that is full of mercy. You are merciful to people that have problems and weakness, even failure. God, you are merciful. Your love never changes. Let them know Your love. Set them free from a performance mentality. In Jesus' name. Amen.

Chapter 13
Rejection and Ministry

The Pastor's wife left the Church in tears. *"Why don't the people appreciate what we do for them?"* she thought. Not a single person thanked her today. She gave some very helpful suggestions to the people in charge of various ministries, but they did things differently than she suggested! *"It's obvious that they hate me,"* she fumed. She was sure she had seen a few people give her strange looks in Church, which made her angry. On the ride home, she raged to her husband, *"If God called us to the ministry, you would think He could at least give us some grateful people. I don't think I can keep doing this!"*

That scenario plays out in many Pastors and Pastor's wives worldwide. The reason the ministry is so painful for them and so many Pastoral couples leave the ministry is that they have brought their unhealed rejection issues into it. This is also true of people who get involved in any ministry in the Church.

Faulty Views of Ministry

Those who bring a performance mentality into serving God view ministry incorrectly.

They view ministry as medicine: People who feel insecure or unloved because of rejection often think, *"If I get involved in ministry, the ministry will fix me!"* They make false assumptions about ministry:
- They think people will appreciate their efforts in ministry: *"I'm sure they'll thank me and always be grateful for my help."*

- They think people will support them and help as they minister: *"I'm sure everyone will agree with every decision I make."*
- They think people will clap, cheer at all they do, and say, *"You are Wonderful!"*

They assume the result of their involvement in ministry will be that they will no longer feel insecure, unloved, or worth less!

- They can view being a Pastor this way: *If people call me "Pastor," if I can give a report at a conference, if my face is on a flyer or website, if I could be an area leader, then I will be healed: I will no longer feel rejected and insecure.*

They view ministry as a way to <u>prove</u> their worth or value: Some rejected people fight the message of rejection they have received, so they become driven to <u>prove</u> their worth.

- Outside of salvation, their attitude is, *"I'll show you I am important. Look at me now!"*

They use money, sports, or achievements to prove their worth.

- But we can bring that attitude into involvement in ministry in the church and ministry for God.
  - They think if they work with new converts, the Pastor will see how wonderful they are:
    - That can create conflict with other people in Church: *Stay away from 'my' converts!*
  - They think, "Look how much I do in the Church. Look how many ministries I'm in." They want other people to ask, "What would we do without you?"

They view ministry as a way to make God love them: They think, *"If I am involved in ministry and being a blessing to other people, God will be pleased with my sacrifice and obedience."*

- The way they think God will show His pleasure: *He will bless me and make my ministry a fantastic success.* But this sets them up for disappointment and bitterness when God doesn't run life according to our self-designed ministry plans.

The Damage of a Performance Mentality in Ministry

These wrong attitudes are very harmful, both to us and the people we minister to.

You will be very unhappy: Not only are the ideas listed above incorrect, but they also contradict what happens in life and ministry.
- Ministry doesn't fix anything wrong in your life—it <u>magnifies</u> it! People in ministry with unhealed rejection wounds perceive every person and every event as a vote on their worth.
- The reality of ministry is that people often don't appreciate you and your efforts. They criticize what you decide and do. They are slow to change. They can disrespect you.

  As a Pastor I work extremely hard on sermons and teaching to feed the people well. But I have people in our Church who sleep through every single sermon! Imagine: *My sermons!* They have probably only heard about 2-1/2 sermons in almost twenty years. So, if I am basing my worth on their response, I probably would have left the ministry to sell insurance long ago!
- The simple truth of ministry is that you often don't get the results you expected. Some Pastors have fewer numbers, less attention, and less money than they thought they would receive in ministry by now.

You can wind up doing damage to other people:
- If you view new converts as the means to your worth – you can push too hard, and give them too much too soon.

UNDERSTANDING

Ministry doesn't fix anything wrong in your life—it <u>magnifies</u> it!

Genesis 33:13 NCV But Jacob said to him, "My master, you know that the children are weak. And I must be careful with my flocks and their young ones. If I force them to go too far in one day, all the animals will die."

Rejected people will tell a brand-new convert six hundred things the convert needs to do to be a 'real Christian.'

Rejected people get upset when new converts miss church: "What do you mean you missed Church because your mother had a heart attack and is dying in the hospital? Are you serious about serving God or not?"

If we treat new converts this way, it shows that it's not about <u>them</u> – it's about <u>us</u>!

Rejected Pastors and wives can do this to the people in their congregation: They constantly get upset, angry, demanding, and even abusive at times because their people are not doing enough!

"You're making me look bad! You're not giving me the validation that I'm seeking!"

You can become embittered at God: The plain fact of life and ministry is that sometimes things don't go well! Early in my ministry, I had a good run of 'success.' A man told me, *"You have the Midas touch – everything you touch turns to gold."* That made me feel great! But shortly after, I developed 'the manure touch' – everything I touched turned to..." You get the idea.

Luke 15:29 NCV But the older son said to his father, 'I have served you like a slave for many years and have always obeyed your commands. But you never gave me even a young goat to have at a feast with my friends.'

The Elder Brother was laboring for his father but getting bitter because he wasn't giving him what he felt he deserved. The goat and feast speak of how he thought he would be publicly recognized, thanked, and praised for his faithful labors. The fact he didn't get those embittered him. He was separated from his father and resentful of the attention his prodigal brother was getting.

People can feel the same way toward their Heavenly Father: *You never gave me great success. You haven't done something great for me that would cause others to celebrate me!* A man who became a missionary (that is good) was not pleased with the lack of appreciation he and his wife received from others. He said, "*I thought missionaries would be treated like heroes!*"

Ministry and Envy

If you're in ministry for the wrong reasons: To fix what's broken in you, to prove your worth, or to make God love you-the natural result will be that **you will resent other people!** I am speaking about resenting other people in the church, other people in ministry.

• You will see other people getting what you feel you need, what you feel you deserve, and what you wish you had.

Other people get opportunities to be seen and recognized.

Other people will do well, and people will applaud them! You will hear people saying nice things about others!

- This produces **Envy**: *Envy is pain or displeasure at other people's blessings, opportunities, and advantages.*

We can have reasons why we're unhappy with their blessings: *We've been saved longer and do more. We're nicer. We're more spiritual.*

Matthew 20:12 NCV They said, 'Those people were hired last and worked only one hour. But you paid them the same as you paid us who worked hard all day in the hot sun. '

Envy causes us to find flaws: *We tell people, "I don't like them, because they're so fake. They're unspiritual. I hear they have a bad marriage. I hear they are mean to puppies..."*

Proverbs 23:6 KJV Eat thou not the bread of him that hath an evil eye...

But it's not actually about them: *It's about what's in our hearts!* An evil eye is viewing people with an envious eye. The mistake of envy is thinking that making other people smaller in worth makes us larger in worth! That is wrong thinking: If you drive an old, beat-up VW Beetle, and you see your neighbor has a new Mercedes, so you decide to take a hammer and smash the Mercedes as much as you can. When you get finished smashing your neighbor's Mercedes – **YOU ARE STILL DRIVING AN OLD, BEAT-UP VW BEETLE!** Smashing your neighbor's car didn't magically make your car more valuable. In the same way, finding flaws with other people doesn't give you more worth!

CHAPTER 13 —— KEY **UNDERSTANDING**

Finding flaws with other people doesn't give you more worth!

1 Samuel 18:8-9 NIV Saul was very angry; this refrain galled him. "They have credited David with tens of thousands," he thought, "but me with only thousands. What more can he get but the kingdom?" ⁹And from that time on Saul kept a jealous eye on David.

We view other people who are on the same team – as <u>competitors</u>! We view them as rivals for attention and rivals for a sense of value.

Mark 9:34 NCV But the followers did not answer, because their argument on the road was about which one of them was the greatest.

Years ago, there was a man who took a dislike to me from the time I was young. He would mistreat me, work against me, speak badly about me, and rally others to also dislike or work against me. I couldn't understand what I had done or said that caused such hatred. One day, I asked his close friend, *"Why does this guy hate me so much?"* He said, *"Sibling rivalry."* I was mystified. I said, *"But we're not siblings!"* He said, *"Exactly – and that's the problem. He wishes he was Pastor Mitchell's son."*

I can fix things if the problem is what I've said or done, but I can't fix envy. That is something deep in the hearts of others.

The Damage of Envy

Envy produces so many unhealthy things in people.
- **Envy produces unhappiness:** People battling envy are never happy. They spend their lives assessing and comparing themselves with others.

- **Envy produces distraction:** When Jesus was telling Peter in John 21 about his future, his question was, *"What's John going to get?"*

> *John 21:22 NCV Jesus answered, "If I want him to live until I come back, that is not your business. You follow me."*

- **Envy produces conflict:**

> *James 4:1-2 NCV Do you know where your fights and arguments come from? They come from the selfish desires that war within you. ²You want things, but you do not have them. So you are ready to kill and are jealous of other people, but you still cannot get what you want. So you argue and fight. You do not get what you want, because you do not ask God.*

Ministry does not heal rejection!

Healing The Performance Mentality in Ministry

Look at the path to healing the performance mentality in ministry:

You must begin with God's love:

> *John 21:15 NLT After breakfast Jesus asked Simon Peter, "Simon son of John, do you love me more than these?" "Yes, Lord," Peter replied, "you know I love you." "Then feed my lambs," Jesus told him.*

This scripture shows us how Jesus treats people after failure: God cares about you despite what you are- despite what you've done!

Mark 16:7 NKJV But go, tell his disciples and Peter, 'He is going ahead of you into Galilee. There you will see him, just as he told you.'

God wants to help you. That is entirely unconnected to your performance.

John 21:5-6 NIV He called out to them, "Friends, haven't you any fish?" "No," they answered. ⁶He said, "Throw your net on the right side of the boat and you will find some." When they did, they were unable to haul the net in because of the large number of fish.

Who was Jesus concerned about? Who was blessed with food? Who is He taking the time to meet with? His followers who had failed. His followers who had not done right! **Yet He still loved them!**

You must focus on loving God, not performing:

John 21:17 NLT A third time he asked him, "Simon son of John, do you love me?" Peter was hurt that Jesus asked the question a third time. He said, "Lord, you know everything. You know that I love you." Jesus said, "Then feed my sheep."

This text gives the correct motivation for ministry: We minister to others because we love God, not to fix what's wrong inside, not to prove our worth, and not as a competition with others.

You must deal with your envy toward others:

John 21:15 NLT After breakfast Jesus asked Simon Peter, "Simon son of John, do you love me more than these?" "Yes, Lord,"

Peter replied, "you know I love you." "Then feed my lambs," Jesus told him.

Jesus is very directly challenging his wrong attitudes in the past: *Do you love me more than the other disciples?* Peter said, *"No. I love You."* Jesus wanted Peter to repent: to change his heart and faulty way of thinking.

The Blessing of Healing

When we deal with the issues in our hearts, it releases good things <u>in</u> us, <u>through</u> us and <u>for</u> us.
- It brings healing and health to our hearts.
- It makes ministry bearable and enjoyable.
- It enables us to help people. We are much more effective at helping people when we are not viewing people as a way to gain self-worth.
- It releases the blessing of God.

Psalm 133:1-3 NKJV Behold, how good and how pleasant it is For brethren to dwell together in unity! 2 It is like the precious oil upon the head, Running down on the beard, The beard of Aaron, Running down on the edge of his garments. 3 It is like the dew of Hermon, Descending upon the mountains of Zion; For there the LORD commanded the blessing-- Life forevermore.

Greg Mitchell
Greg Mitchell - Rejection Testimony

Greg Mitchell
Chapter 13 - Rejection and Ministry

Prayer: I want to pray for you that God will help you with rejection issues to make you effective in ministry.

God, I am asking first of all for disciples that are watching this, or people who feel they may be called to the ministry, that have rejection issues. I need You to open their eyes. I'm asking You to bring healing in their hearts. Give them revelation. Let them be healed now, so when they enter into their destiny, they can be effective for You. God, there are pastors and pastor's wives right now, that may be watching or reading or listening. I need You to do miracles in them. They already are in the ministry. They already are facing battles, that the source flows out of rejection. They need a healing. God, I rebuke every lying spirit that would cloud their mind and cause them to not see clearly, open their eyes and enable them to see Your will. Let them know Your love, and bring healing from rejection. Lord God. The wounds of the past will be healed. Enable them to forgive and let them know Your love. Every person, God make us able ministers of the Gospel, so we can do that for You and bless other people. And I thank You for what You're going to do. In Jesus name. Amen.

Chapter 14
Rejection and Body Image

"I don't want to look like a freak; I just want to look a little bit better." I was getting a haircut in a salon that also did ladies' hair. There was only one other customer, so while the man cut my hair, I could hear the other female hairdresser speaking to her client. They were discussing Botox and plastic surgery and the various benefits of it. My wife has never had any of it done, so I had no idea why ladies think these are good options. Then I heard the hairdresser say those words, *"I don't want to look like a freak; I just want to look a little bit better."* Her client agreed. This made me want to see what they looked like. In the mirror, I could see both of them already had numerous procedures, and their features, to my eyes, were already changing in various ways. It made me doubt that she would be happy with looking *"a little bit better."*

That event revealed a problem that unhealed rejection causes: *Unhappiness with your own body.*

Body Image

Two of our society's idols are <u>beauty</u> and <u>body</u>. The constant message we hear is that your worth and your value are based on your looks and your body. Think about advertising: *How often do you see ugly people advertising a product?* This is often subliminal in advertising: *Buy this car, and you'll look like the people in the ad. You'll get the kind of girl or guy you see in the ad.*

We take in constant messaging about beauty and our bodies:

- Advertising: A lot of advertising is inspired by hell! Ads are deliberately designed to make you feel inferior and unhappy with yourself so you will buy their product!
- Movies and TV: They are filled with beautiful people. Behind the scenes in movies and TV, people are paid to make the actors look good.
- Social media: It is incredibly destructive. You can look at photos of other people online (some of which are faked, filtered, or photoshopped) and inevitably compare yourself to them. This produces insecurity.

Rejection is often focused on our bodies: In the past, someone told us we were not acceptable based on our bodies or our looks. Perhaps you were mocked or told, *"You're too short, too tall, too fat, too thin, you look strange in glasses, you look strange with braces, your teeth are crooked, your nose is too big,"*...on and on. Children often created cruel nicknames that centered on our bodies.

The lie is that your worth is based on your looks or based on your body. People think, *"If I looked like that, I would be valuable, and people would love me."*
- Your worth is based on looks? The standard of beauty has changed through the years. Beautiful women in the middle ages would be considered fat today.
- Your worth is based on bra size? That is demeaning, no matter what the size.
- Your worth is based on something that will not last. *Beautiful people won't always look like that!* Age and gravity always win.
- Your body and your looks are not an accurate indicator of your worth.

Proverbs 11:22 NLT *A beautiful woman who lacks discretion is like a gold ring in a pig's snout.*

If you put beautiful jewelry on a female pig, *she's still a pig!*

Every person has a body image. Body image is the mental view we hold concerning our appearance. Most of us focus on the <u>flaws</u> we have in our bodies or our looks. When we look in the mirror or look at photos of ourselves, we tend to see what we feel is not good about our body shape, nose, eyes, hair, etc.

- Billions are spent each year on fitness: Not for health, but for looks. But we are often striving for an unattainable ideal. We are trying for the perfection we saw in a model's body or an athlete's body. We don't take into account genetics: *Sometimes, it is impossible to look like that!*
- Billions are spent on cosmetic surgery. *Americans spent $20.1 billion dollars on cosmetic surgery procedures in 2020.* For women, this was for procedures for their lips, eyes, skin, tummy, breasts, etc. But men also are getting facial procedures and implants on their pecs and calves.

This obsession with body image is demonic: ***Demon spirits tell you you're not acceptable!***

1 John 4:18 NKJV There is no fear in love; but perfect love casts out fear, because fear involves torment. But he who fears has not been made perfect in love.

CHAPTER 14 —— KEY UNDERSTANDING

Obsession with body image is demonic. Demon spirits tell you you're not acceptable!

Self-rejection and Negative Body Image

People who have not dealt with rejection can wind up rejecting themselves.

- **We often speak against our bodies:** We say, *"I hate my legs, my lips, my nose..."*
- **We go to incredible lengths to try and change our looks or bodies:** We try to do this through fitness obsession or surgery.
    The mistaken idea behind this is, *"If I could fix this/that - <u>THEN</u> I would be acceptable, or <u>THEN</u> I would be happy with my looks!"* But that's not true! It's not logical; it's demonic.

I was preaching in Melbourne, Australia, when a girl in her twenties came and spoke to me after the service. She felt her hips and her outer thigh stuck out a bit. She was anorexic, and dieting made her thin to an unhealthy level, but dieting didn't change the shape of her bones. She pointed to her hip bone and said, *"If I could just get surgery and have them shave off the bone right there (she pointed to the bone), I would be happy!"*

The Damage of a Negative Body Image

A negative body image causes damage in many ways:
- **Negative body image makes you unhappy:** When we give in to the lie of body image, we fall into the trap of comparison: *They're thinner, they're prettier, they're more fit, they're better looking...* It is a scientifically proven fact that social media causes unhappiness and depression!
- **Negative body image affects relationships:** When we give in to the lie of body image, we pull away from others because we are convinced they wouldn't like someone like us. We don't give ourselves entirely to others, because we think, *"They're*

going to see my flaws and reject me. They're going to find someone else that looks better." In marriage, women with negative body image tend to withhold themselves, and men with negative body image tend to criticize.

- **Negative body image makes you vulnerable:** If your rejection is based on your looks, then you become vulnerable to flattery. You open yourself mentally and emotionally to someone who tells you, *"You're beautiful"* or *"You're handsome."*

> **Proverbs 7:21 NLT** *So she seduced him with her pretty speech and enticed him with her flattery.*

- **Negative body image can actually make you sick:** Naomi Judd said, *"Your body hears everything your mind says."* This is scientifically accurate: Your words affect your body on a cellular level. But this is more than science - this is spiritual! The Bible tells us that God hears your words! You say, *"God, please heal my body..."* The same body He hears you say bad things about?

Wonderfully Made

Psalm 139 gives us the truth about our bodies.

- **God was involved in your creation:** The lie from hell is that you were a mistake, an accident, an inconvenience. But that is not what <u>God </u>says!

> **Psalm 139:13 NKJV** *For You formed my inward parts; You covered me in my mother's womb.*
> The word "covered" means to knit and weave. This tells us we were planned and then formed.

- **God says your body is wonderful.**

    Psalm 139:14 NKJV *I will praise You, for I am fearfully and wonderfully made; Marvelous are Your works, And that my soul knows very well.*

    Marvelous means 'extraordinary', or 'awesome.' *Marvelous are your works:* Which works? **Our bodies!** God says that our bodies are extraordinary and awesome – to Him! Our false opinions are based on the lies of the world.

- **God has plans for your life – that includes your body!**

Our True Value

Your worth and value have <u>nothing</u> to do with your looks or your body!

    Psalm 139:17-18 NKJV [17]*How precious also are Your thoughts to me, O God! How great is the sum of them!* [18]*If I should count them, they would be more in number than the sand; When I awake, I am still with You.*

    This verse is amazing because it shows that God is thinking about you! *He is thinking good thoughts about you!*

CHAPTER 14 —— KEY   UNDERSTANDING

Your worth and value have <u>nothing</u> to do with your looks or your body!

Jeremiah 29:11 NKJV For I know the thoughts that I think toward you, says the Lord, thoughts of peace and not of evil, to give you a future and a hope.

You are loved – regardless of how you look or what your body is like! So, how should we react in light of this truth?

- **We must repent for rejecting our body that God created:** We need to pray and tell God, *"I am sorry for rejecting what you say is wonderful and beautiful. That is not acceptable to You."*
- **We need to take authority over the tormenting spirits that lie about our bodies and lie about our worth!**

Luke 9:1 NKJV Jesus called the twelve apostles together and gave them power and authority over all demons and the ability to heal sicknesses.

- **We must speak differently about our bodies:**

Proverbs 18:21 NIV The tongue has the power of life and death, and those who love it will eat its fruit.

Thank God for your body! Say what God says about your body.

Testimony: Ever since I was little, some family members and people had always rejected me, whom I thought were my friends. I was never wanted in friend groups that were my own age, and people I wanted to be around would tease and mock me for being different. As a young teenager, I had some friends, but they were very selective about when they wanted me around. I was constantly told I was too sheltered and that I was never going to fit in with everyone else. I was gossiped about and was never invited to gatherings, hangouts, or special events.

I got to the point where I felt so alone and rejected that I started to have suicidal thoughts. I couldn't function normally because I was constantly being rejected. I was already saved, but I knew these thoughts were poisoning my mind, so I decided I needed to pray and ask Jesus to help me. Jesus delivered me from the depression and suicidal thoughts I was having. I was still rejected by people, even after I prayed.

When I was sixteen, Pastor Greg started his Sunday School, Uprooting Rejection. I was still dealing with rejection and feeling unworthy of people's acceptance. I listened to that first Sunday School lesson, and everything changed. I went and listened to every lesson about Uprooting Rejection. Pastor Greg led us in many prayers during the series, rebuking the devil's lies and asking God to set us free from rejection. I felt a weight lift off of me, and God set me free from rejection.

I finally felt accepted in a way I had never felt before, and I found a joy in my salvation that I hadn't had before. I am loved by the God who created me.

Greg Mitchell
Chapter 14 – Rejection and body image

Prayer: Some of you have seen how rejection has affected your view of your own body and your worth, so I want to pray for you.

God, there are people that they have believed a lie. That their worth depends on their looks and on their body; that is a lie from hell. Some of these people have been driven in unhealthy ways, they're seeking to emulate the idols of the world when our world worships looks and bodies, that's from hell. God, set them free. There are people here, they have spoken against the body that You've given them. God help them to understand how You view them, and then let them view their body in a healthy way. We have been fearfully and wonderfully made. And so, God help people to accept flaws, break the curse of words that they've spoken about their own bodies, and help them to see themselves clearly. Their worth comes from You. It does not come from their looks. It does not come from their bodies. I thank You for Your love. In Jesus' name. Amen.

Chapter 15 Healing Rejection Part 1

"It was like a fog lifted from my mind," he said. "Growing up with rejection, I didn't realize how it affected how I saw everything. When I came into a new class, a new job, or later, when I came into Church, the moment I walked in, I was looking at people and wondering how they would reject me – and they did. I didn't realize I was interpreting everything from a faulty viewpoint. I was seeing every look and hearing every word with offense. I was sure people were looking at me in strange ways. I just knew they were talking bad about me. When people said anything to me, I would quickly take offense; 'What did you mean by that?' I spent half the time being angry and ready to fight and the other half offended and wanting to run. It was a miserable way to live."

"But, when I understood that rejection was producing these reactions in me, I cried out to God to set me free from the spirit of rejection and the fear of rejection. It was like a fog lifted from my mind, and now I no longer look at people the same way. I felt different, so I didn't hear and interpret things with offense. It has transformed my relationships and my relationship with God. I am grateful for God's power to heal and deliver."

That is the hope of the Gospel: freedom from the past and deliverance in our lives now. For the next two chapters, we will examine the process of healing from rejection.

Healing The Past

The hope of the Gospel and serving God is freedom from the past! The past does not determine your future. You are not doomed because of past rejection.

Luke 4:18-19 NLT [18]*"The Spirit of the Lord is upon me, for he has anointed me to bring Good News to the poor. He has sent me to proclaim that captives will be released, that the blind will see, that the oppressed will be set free,* [19]*and that the time of the Lord's favor has come."*

Jesus was announcing the good news of the results of Jesus coming into your life: *You don't have to stay the way you are!* There is freedom from painful emotions and destructive thinking patterns. Jesus sets captives free! God promises that whoever wants to have a new future can!

Isaiah 43:19 NIV See, I am doing a new thing! Now it springs up; do you not perceive it? I am making a way in the desert and streams in the wasteland.

1 Chronicles 4:10 NIV Jabez cried out to the God of Israel, "Oh, that you would bless me and enlarge my territory! Let your hand be with me, and keep me from harm so that I will be free from pain." And God granted his request.

CHAPTER 15 —— KEY ⚷ UNDERSTANDING

The hope of the Gospel and serving God is freedom from the past!

We need supernatural healing from the past. Rejection does damage inside spiritually and emotionally. Rejection has painful emotions attached to it. I can't <u>talk</u> you out of your pain: **You need a supernatural miracle of healing!**

*Luke 4:18 NKJV "The Spirit of the Lord is upon Me, Because He has anointed Me To preach the gospel to the poor; **He has sent Me to heal the brokenhearted,** To proclaim liberty to the* *captives And recovery of sight to the blind, To set at liberty those who are oppressed;"*

To those whose hearts have been broken by being actively rejected or never receiving the love and approval you needed: *You can be healed!*

Genesis 41:51 NKJV *Joseph called the name of the firstborn Manasseh (forgetting): "For God has made me forget all my toil and all my father's house."*

Joseph was rejected and violated by his brothers. But years later, he names his first son Manasseh, which means 'Forgetting.' He was publicly saying, *"It doesn't hurt anymore! My past pain is now simply information."*

In the Parable of the Good Samaritan, the Samaritan poured oil and wine into the wounds of the man attacked by thieves. He applied healing to the places where the man was hurting. Oil was a symbol of the Holy Spirit. That tells us God can apply the Holy Spirit to your broken heart!

Psalm 147:3 NKJV *He heals the brokenhearted And binds up their wounds.*

Isaiah 53:3-5 NKJV *He is despised and rejected by men, A Man of sorrows and acquainted with grief. And we hid, as it were, our faces from Him; He was despised, and we did not esteem Him.* 4 *Surely He has borne our griefs And carried our sorrows; Yet we esteemed Him stricken, Smitten by God, and afflicted.* 5 *But He was wounded for our transgressions, He was bruised for our iniquities; The chastisement for our peace was upon Him, And by His stripes we are healed.*

Because Jesus was despised and rejected, He can heal those who have been rejected.

A Supernatural Deliverance

Healing the past involves a supernatural deliverance. A lesson we learn from Jesus healing people in the New Testament: Sometimes what is affecting you is demonic. *It is from hell!*

> **Matthew 8:16 NCV** *That evening people brought to Jesus many who had demons. Jesus spoke and the demons left them, and he healed all the sick.*

Rejection is partly demonic. There are tormenting spirits of fear, shame, paranoia, and the fear of rejection.

> **Luke 9:1 NKJV** *Jesus called the twelve apostles together and gave them power and authority over all demons and the ability to heal sicknesses.*

If you are a Christian, you don't have to live tormented by those spirits anymore: *You have the power to cast those spirits out!*

CHAPTER 15 —— KEY ⚷ UNDERSTANDING

Healing the past involves a supernatural deliverance.

Participating in Your Own Rescue

If you want to uproot rejection, you must forgive those who rejected you. When people hurt us by rejecting us, it is normal to feel angry at their rejection: *Why would you treat* *me like that? Why wouldn't you give me what I needed? It's not fair!*

But sometimes people <u>hold on</u> to past offenses: This is called resentment or bitterness.

Hebrews 12:15 NLT *...Watch out that no poisonous root of bitterness grows up to trouble you, corrupting many.*

- Rejected people are often still fighting with those who reject them: *They are taking out their anger on others today.*
- Rejected people often try to prove things to those who rejected them.

As long as you hold on to anger and resentment, the people who rejected you continue to have power over you.

Matthew 18:34-35 NCV [34]*The master was very angry and put the servant in prison to be punished until he could pay everything he owed.* [35]*"This king did what my heavenly Father will do to you if you do not forgive your brother or sister from your heart."*

The one who failed to repay him now has the power keep him in prison!

How long will you allow people from your past to ruin your life, your relationships, and your relationship with God?

Get a calendar and pick a date when you will let it go. Will you let them have power over you for another six months? Will you let them have power over you for another five years? That's not just foolish; it's sick!

So, the only logical answer is to <u>forgive</u>: **To release the debt.** *"They owe me love. They owe me my childhood that was stolen."* **Let it go!**

Ephesians 4:32 NCV Be kind and loving to each other, and <u>forgive each other</u> just as God forgave you in Christ.

To forgive is to recognize, *I am not the judge. <u>My</u> part is to let it go. <u>God's</u> part is to heal.*

Forgiveness allows God to do a miracle <u>in</u> us, and <u>for</u> us.

Mark 11:24-25 NLT 24"I tell you, you can pray for anything, and if you believe that you've received it, it will be yours. 25But when you are praying, first forgive anyone you are holding a grudge against, so that your Father in heaven will forgive your sins, too."

An essential part of forgiveness is changing the way we speak. Rejected people often retell the rejections and violations from their past. They often retell their painful past to excuse their current behavior. When they are in conflict, or someone confronts them about unacceptable behavior or attitudes, they often retell their pain: *"I act that way because of how I was raised. Of course, I talk this way – you don't know what they said to me!"* **Whatever you speak out, you keep alive!** If you no longer want the past to keep damaging your life in the present, stop speaking about it! The sign that we have genuinely forgiven people is when we stop retelling their violations.

If you want to uproot rejection, you must reject rejection. Jesus didn't agree with the Jews' or the Romans' opinion of Him.

John 8:48-50 NIV ⁴⁸*The Jews answered him, "Aren't we right in saying that you are a Samaritan and demon-possessed?"* ⁴⁹*"I am not possessed by a demon," said Jesus, "but I honor my Father and you dishonor me.* ⁵⁰*I am not seeking glory for myself; but there is one who seeks it, and he is the judge."*

In our lives, we have received opinions of rejection and worth from people or from hell. Sometimes, we accept that opinion as true, or we accept the feelings of rejection as normal. Accepting these blocks us from hearing the truth and blocks God's blessings.

What we need to do is break agreement with rejection: Deliberately reject the lies of who we are and the lies of who we are not.

Numbers 30:3, 5 NKJV ³*Or if a woman makes a vow to the Lord, and binds herself by some agreement while in her father's house in her youth,* ⁵*But if her father overrules her on the day that he hears, then none of her vows nor her agreements by which she has bound herself shall stand; and the Lord will release her, because her father overruled her.*

This verse was the Old Testament provision for those who had spoken words that bound them somehow. God made a way to break the power of those words off a person's life.

This speaks of our privilege in prayer. We can get very specific about words that have been spoken over us or against us by others. It also may involve unhealthy words we have spoken over ourselves in our pain.

- We can pray specifically: *Those words of rejection spoken to me - I reject them! Unhealthy words I have spoken over myself - I break the curse of those words.*
- We can battle in prayer against assaults from hell. These often come as negative feelings that torment us. We can pray against them: *These feelings are not normal - they're from hell, and I cast them out and command them to leave!*

*Chuck Dean spoke to 200 Vietnam veterans. He told them of the destructive power of bitterness and how he had forgiven Jane Fonda for betraying the US during the Vietnam War. He asked who wanted to be free from this woman and what she represented to them. Many hands shot up into the air. The exit door banged open as he prayed for these men's deliverance. He saw a big Marine named Rob in his wheelchair hurriedly wheel from the room. About an hour later, Rob, who had not been out of his wheelchair for 20 years, walked in the door! Rob said, "I decided to give in and prayed that God would help me to forgive Jane Fonda. When I said that prayer, my legs suddenly tingled with feeling. The sensation in my legs scared me so much that I went straight to the VA hospital to have them checked out. After probing around, they discovered that I had feelings in my legs. **So, I got up and walked out, leaving my wheelchair behind!**" Then, with evident gratitude, he added, "Not only am I free from her, but I'm free from my wheelchair, too!"*

That is what God wants to do for you. Forgive so you can be free from the people who have rejected you and allow miracle power to flow into your life.

Testimony: I will describe my life in a nutshell without going into details or describing events because otherwise, it would be a very long story. I was born in a hospital in India and immediately taken to an orphanage. I lived there until I was five. The people working in the orphanage believed in corporal punishment and liked to use it.

Then, I was adopted by a Dutch family with a father, mother, and two older brothers. My father was an alcoholic and a workaholic and was, therefore, absent. My eldest brother is physically disabled and requires a lot of care and attention. He bullied me since I arrived, and as a child, I found it challenging to deal with him. My other brother is their biological child and, therefore, loved by my adoptive mother.

I did not live up to my adoptive mother's expectations. That was because, in her opinion, I was rebellious and disobedient. This resulted in her physical and psychological abuse, humiliation, and neglect from the age of five to the age of thirty-one. The mental abuse even continued when I left home at age twenty-one. I had several emotional breakdowns. During my breakdowns, I had suicidal thoughts and was depressed, angry, and bitter.

I then encountered spirituality. The person who started reading my soul told me things she could not have known from my youth. I believed in that, then. I then trained to read souls and auras myself. At one point, I wanted to read someone, but I was blocked. When I asked the force blocking me who he was. I was told clearly that it was God. And God said, "This person is mine, and you stay away from him." I wasn't a Christian, and I didn't believe it. Then I tried again and got the same message again. After that, I stopped being a reader of souls and auras.

Six months later, I was converted at the Door church. Later, God convinced me to forgive my mother. I didn't want to because she didn't deserve it. But the conviction remained and even

Chris Thorne
Salvation Story

Leebon Britoe
First time I heard I was loved

became stronger. After a year and a half, I forgave and blessed my adoptive mother.

My adoptive mother unfortunately passed away fourteen months ago. I am very happy I took the step to forgive and bless her because I was stuck in my past. I thought then that I was done with my past. But I was still afraid; I was desperate to survive. I always felt unwanted, unloved, unsafe, and distrusted by everyone. I have had several therapies but noticed that it did not help.

In November 2023, I heard Pastor Greg's Bible study on uprooting rejection. I recognized in myself more than 75% of everything that was mentioned in the Bible study. By praying during the series, I noticed that I am less afraid and no longer feel rejected so easily. I also feel more love from God and can recognize the holy spirit is working on me. I realize more and more that God is trustworthy and loving and that He will never leave me. I have noticed that I have a more positive outlook on life and feel love for myself and others. I testify more and want to tell others about Jesus. I also notice that I am a kinder wife to my husband and a more loving mother to my two-year-old daughter.

I haven't had that much happiness in my life up until God delivered me, but now, when I think about God, pray, sing, or read the Bible, I honestly feel a joy I have never had before. That is why I am so grateful for this Bible study and what God is doing in my life.

Greg Mitchell
Chapter 15 – Healing from Rejection – part 1

Prayer: Now that God has opened your eyes, we're going to begin the process of praying for healing, and I want to pray for you right now.

God, there are people here that they need more than words. They need a miracle. First, I am asking for supernatural healing.

God, You said that Jesus Christ came to heal the broken hearted. There are people - their hearts have been broken by rejection. They need a miracle of healing. God, apply the oil of the Holy Spirit. Heal every wound, every word that was spoken in the past. I break that curse of words off of them. Heal their hearts. God there are people that are bound in anger and resentment. God, they're filled with bitterness over past rejections. Enable them right now to truly forgive from their heart. The past will no longer rule their lives anymore. As they are able to let it go, do a miracle in their hearts and God, I pray that You are going to supernaturally enable them to find deliverance. I take authority over rejection and the fear of rejection. I cast it out from their hearts and their minds, set the captives free right now they are going to experience healing, forgiveness and deliverance, from this moment on. In Jesus' name. Amen.

Chapter 16
Healing Rejection Part 2

In 2016, a high school teacher in Colorado named Brittni Darras found out that one of her best students had come very close to committing suicide. Darras was heartbroken to think that one of her students could be so sad that she would consider taking her own life. So Darras asked the girl's mother if she could write her daughter a letter. In the letter, Brittni Darras told the girl what she saw when she looked at her. She saw a young woman with a great personality and intellect, and a bright future. When the girl received the letter, she remarked to her mother, "I didn't think anyone would say such nice things to me. I didn't think anyone would miss me when I'm gone."

The letter had such a positive effect on that young student that Darras wound up writing a personal letter to every single one of her students—all 130 of them—to tell them all the good things she saw in them. She gave them out to each student before they went on summer vacation, prompting hugs and smiles from many of the teens as they read the kind words. One student thrust her letter into the air and said it was the best thing she had ever gotten.

Darras says that her students loved their letters. They read them over and over again, shared them with their friends, and one girl said, "I'm going to keep this forever." They never realized how much they mattered to their teacher, that she saw something special in each one of them.

This story illustrates an important part of healing from rejection: **knowing who you are, which is based on God's love for you.**

CHAPTER 16 — KEY   UNDERSTANDING

Healing from rejection comes from knowing who you are, which is based on God's love for you.

Love Casting Out Fear

Rejection is ultimately an assault on love. Somehow, we were given the message, *"You are not loved, valued, accepted, or worth loving."*

The primary effect of rejection is centered on the issue of love.

- **We are unable to <u>give</u> love:** *Do you say "I love you" to your family or your spouse? Can you express love, appreciation, value, and affection?*
- **We cannot <u>receive</u> love:** *When rejected people get compliments from others, they don't believe it. Rejected people are uncomfortable with love and affection.*
- **Rejected people live with uncertainty:** They are never certain or confident in human relationships and relationship with God. They always have thoughts nagging at the back of their minds; *I'm not good enough. He wouldn't like me. They wouldn't like me.*

The answer for rejection is love! We don't heal rejection by looking at the source of <u>rejection</u> but by looking at the source of <u>love</u>.

1 John 4:18 NKJV There is no fear in love; but perfect love casts out fear, because fear involves torment. But he who fears has not been made perfect in love.

Ultimately everything depends on the basis of Christianity: **God's love.**

1 John 4:16 NKJV And we have known and believed the love that God has for us. God is love, and he who abides in love abides in God, and God in him.

God wants to have relationship with you! *1 John 4:19 NKJV We love Him because He first loved us.*

The God of the universe was not happy to live without us: *God came out of heaven to bring us into His family.* God made an incredible effort and paid the highest price so you could be included in His family.

1 John 3:1 NKJV Behold, what manner of love the Father hath bestowed upon us, that we should be called the sons of God:

God's love is not deserved or earned – it is <u>given</u>: *1 John 4:19 NKJV...He <u>first</u> loved us!*
- For those who feel they don't measure up: God knew what He was getting when He invited you to be part of His family.
- For those who think their problems will cause God to change His mind about us: He wants to help you when you have problems!

Ephesians 1:6-7 NKJV ⁶to the praise of the glory of His grace, by which He has made us accepted in the Beloved. ⁷ In Him we have redemption through His blood, the forgiveness of sins, according to the riches of His grace

This verse says two very powerful statements:

It says we are <u>accepted</u>: The word means *'To give special honor. To be highly favored.'* It is not just that God <u>tolerates</u> us; it is that we are special, honored, and favored in His eyes.

It says we are <u>in the beloved</u>: This means that we are viewed like <u>Jesus</u> was viewed! We are loved like <u>Jesus</u> was. We are not just followers – we are a part of God's family!

CHAPTER 16 —— KEY UNDERSTANDING

The answer for rejection is love!

God Delights In You

***Zephaniah 3:17 NCV** The LORD your God is with you; the mighty One will save you. He will rejoice over you. You will rest in his love; he will sing and be joyful about you."*

God gives us a picture of how He views us. He is not merely tolerating us; He is rejoicing over us! Any loving parent or grandparent has a good idea of what this means. When my daughter was born, I had to restrain myself from showing complete strangers photos of my daughter. I was absolutely thrilled with her – and she hadn't done anything yet! We made up silly songs to sing to her. We thought every little thing she did was the most wonderful thing that had ever been done. That is how God feels about you! He rejoices over you! Maybe in heaven, he pulls out your photo and says to the angels, *"That's my boy,"* or *"That's my girl!"*

God is glad you're in the family. He doesn't just love you (for God so loved the world) – He likes you! One day, a man in our church made a very honest and powerful statement to me. He said, *"I know that God loves me, but to be honest, I'm not sure that He likes me!"*

Some of you love your extended family. You are okay with getting together with them once or twice a year. But you might not actually like some of them. You don't want them to be a regular part of your life. But God likes you! He wants to be with you. He wants to have a relationship with you!

God Wants to Give You Good Things

Romans 8:32 NKJV *He who did not spare His own Son, but delivered Him up for us all, how shall He not with Him also freely give us all things?*

That verse gives us a very encouraging logic: If God already showed that He would give the most expensive gift ever (His own Son) so we could be in His family, there is no limit to what God is willing to give to the ones He loves!

My wife and I now have grandchildren. We are always <u>looking</u> for ways to bless. If we see toys or sporting equipment, we say, *"Benjamin and Jonathan need those!"* When we see pretty dresses in the store, we say, *"Ellie and Rory need those!"* I'm sure they could live without the things we give them, but we love to give them good things because we love **THEM!**

Whatever need I have in life, whatever situation I face, I think, **"My Heavenly Father loves me!! He will help me!!"** I don't know <u>what</u> He will do to help, I don't know <u>how</u> He will help, but because I know He loves me, I am confident He will help me.

182

Luke 12:32 NKJV Do not fear, little flock; for it is your Father's good pleasure to give you the kingdom.

Those who don't have a revelation of God's love think that prayer is making God do what He doesn't really want to do. But Jesus says we don't have to live in fear because God gets <u>pleasure</u> from giving us good things.

The Blessing of Rest

The Jewish religious system was filled with many rules and rituals people had to follow to be right with God. Those people must have lived with a lot of uncertainty: *Did I miss one of the rules? Did I accidentally touch something unclean that makes me unable to come into God's presence?*

But even Christians who do not understand God's love live in uncertainty and fear. Am I good enough? Have I done enough? Do I measure up, so God won't be unhappy with me? But the Bible makes powerful statements in the New Testament: *"In Christ"* or *"In Him."* These terms speak of how God views us: Because God has given us Jesus' righteousness, God looks at us as being <u>in union</u> with Jesus. That means He sees us not as weak, failing people but as loved and accepted children. When Jesus died on the cross, Jesus last words were, *"It is finished."* The price is paid. We are now accepted and loved by God – based on Jesus' perfect life and sacrifice.

The practical result of our identity in Christ is **rest**.

Hebrews 4:10 NKJV for anyone who enters God's rest also rests from his own work, just as God did from his.

We can rest in God's love, which means we don't have to be afraid, thinking, *"I have to earn, deserve, perform, or measure up in order to have God's love. "*

1 John 4:18 NKJV *There is no fear in love; but perfect love casts out fear.*

In the book "Knowing God," S.J. Hill said, *"You weren't made to find your identity in the stuff you do. You were made to be in relationship with God. The Father doesn't define your life by what you do. He defines your life by who He created you to be for Himself. He doesn't want your efforts as much as He wants you. He enjoys your worship. He enjoys the times that you think about Him. But most of all, He enjoys you."*

CHAPTER 16 —— KEY UNDERSTANDING

The practical result of our identity in Christ is rest.

Possessing God's Love

God's love is an accomplished fact, But you have a personal responsibility to make it real.

You must ask God for a <u>revelation</u> of His love:

Ephesians 3:18-19 NKJV *may be able to comprehend with all the saints what is the width and length and depth and height-- to know the love of Christ which passes knowledge; that you may be filled with all the fullness of God.*

The word 'know' means to experience. If I were to ask you, *"Do you believe God loves you?"* You would probably nod your head and agree, thinking of **John 3:16 NKJV** *For God so loved the world...* But it needs to go from your <u>head</u> to your <u>heart</u>; so it becomes <u>yours</u>! *I know it! I experience it! I feel it!* That is a miracle that God is willing to do for you.

You must document God's love:

The only place you can truly find God's love is in the Bible. I sometimes challenge people to read the Bible and look at Jesus (God in the flesh) and see how He treated people (not the Pharisees!) *What did he say to them? What did he do for them?* Jesus Christ is the revelation of God. What He did for others is what He will do for you! I see him providing for people in need, helping desperate people, and speaking kindly to people who have failed. He will do the same for you!

We need to read, study, and <u>personalize</u> God's word: When you read of a promise God makes, you must say, *"That promise is for <u>me</u>! That is what God wants for <u>me</u>! That is what God will do for <u>me</u>!"*

I have told in the past that when I wanted God's miracle power in my life, I read, studied, and prayed over scriptures that promised miracle healing power. One day in my office, I was reading **Hebrews 13:8 NKJV** *Jesus Christ is the same yesterday, today, and forever.* Suddenly, it became a revelation. It went from my <u>head</u> to my <u>heart</u>! It was <u>mine</u>! From that moment, I knew that healing power would work for me today! You must do that for yourself concerning God's love for you and your identity in Christ.

Write it down: **Habakkuk 2:2 NKJV** *Then the Lord answered me and said: "Write the vision And make it plain on tablets, That he may run who reads it."* There is something powerful about taking the time to write down what God says. That sometimes is the way that information becomes a revelation. I have pages of Bible verses on various situations I was going through at the time. I took the time to write them down and then pray over them. The various promises (healing, money, deliverance, guidance) became a revelation for me.

You must receive God's love by faith: To receive God's love is a choice of faith. You do this the same way you got saved, filled with the Holy Spirit, healed, or financially provided for. You heard what God promised, and you decided, *"It's true, and it's true for <u>me</u>!"*

1 John 4:16 NKJV *we have known <u>and believed</u> the love God has for us...*

Steering Your Heart

The Bible speaks about the power of words.

James 3:4-5 NKJV *⁴Look also at ships: although they are so large and are driven by fierce winds, they are turned by a very small rudder wherever the pilot desires. ⁵Even so the tongue is a little member and boasts great things...*

Your mouth is the rudder of your heart! The rudder of your life. What you say will steer or affect your heart.

Proverbs 18:21 NIV *The tongue has the power of life and death, and those who love it will eat its fruit.*

Words are <u>producing</u> things in your heart and in your life!

- **You must <u>stop</u> saying things <u>against</u> the love of God:** Many people have spent a lifetime saying, *"I'm not good enough, I'm not like other people."* You are saying things opposite to what God says about your worth and your identity.

    It's not an accident that God made Zechariah unable to speak during the term of Elizabeth's pregnancy. God didn't want him to speak words <u>against</u> God's plans for their lives!

- **You must align your mouth with the truth of God's love:** Jesus spoke his identity out loud!

    John 10:30 NCV *"The Father and I are one."*
    John 3:35 NCV *The Father loves the Son and has given him power over everything.*

WHO GOD SAYS I AM: *I am blessed with every spiritual blessing in Christ (Eph 1:3) I was chosen before the foundations of the world. (Eph 1:4) I am called to be holy and without blame in love. (Eph 1:4) I am adopted in Christ to Father God. (Eph 1:5) I am accepted in the family of God. (Eph 1:6) I am forgiven. (Eph 1:7) I have a wonderful inheritance. (Eph 1:11) I am sealed with the Holy Spirit of promise. (Eph 1:13) I have a hope and a calling. (Eph 1:18) I am alive. (Eph 2:1) I am seated in heavenly places with Christ. (Eph 2:6) I am God's workmanship. (Eph 2:10) I am created for good works. (Eph 2:10) I have been brought near to God. (Eph 2:13) I am not separated from God. (Eph 2:14-18) I have access today to the Father! (Eph 2:18)*

The Power of Gratitude

The power of hell is defeated by gratitude and worship: *Vocally thanking God for good things. Who He is. What He has done for us. How He views us.*

Philippians 4:6-7 NLT *⁶Don't worry about anything; instead, pray about everything. Tell God what you need, and thank him for all he has done. ⁷ Then you will experience God's peace, which exceeds anything we can understand. His peace will guard your hearts and minds as you live in Christ Jesus.*

- People who do not know God's love blame and complain. Their attitude and words hinder God's work in their lives.
- People who know God's love worship and thank God.

Worship causes God to come down into our situation and turn things around for our benefit. As Paul and Silas worshipped in the prison, a supernatural earthquake happened causing the prison doors to open and their chains to fall off.

Thankfulness protects us. Philippians 4:6-7 shows that when we *"thank him for all he has done,"* *"His peace will guard our hearts and minds."* 'Guard' is a word picture of a soldier standing sentry and denying access. The Devil is not very successful in attacking and gaining entrance into the hearts and minds of thankful believers.

I am praying that God has opened the eyes of your understanding so that you will experience a genuine deliverance from the spirit of rejection. This will enable you to walk in true freedom as you gain confidence in God's love.

Testimony: Dear Pastor Greg, I first sensed I had an issue with rejection in my teens and early twenties. I often struggled to receive any feedback or correction, and I would take it very personally, nearly always resulting in tears. I would also become very defensive and seek to justify myself and blame others, not accepting personal responsibility. These types of encounters and conflicts in relationships were very emotionally painful for me, and I remember having these issues from primary school age. If I ever made a mistake at school and was reprimanded by my teacher or someone in a position of authority, it would destroy me. I hated feeling that pain, so I strived hard to be perfect and never misstep or make a mistake.

GREG & LISA MITCHELL AND REECE AND MARIAH COOKE

Testimony: I got married at age 21, and by age 24, my husband and I started trying for a family. Here is where things began to unravel. I fell pregnant with an ectopic pregnancy, lost my baby, and effectively lost my fertility all at once. I had emergency surgery, where they removed my right fallopian tube. Later, they discovered my left fallopian tube was also fully blocked, which left me unable to conceive naturally. This rocked my world. My heart desired to be a mother and all I had ever dreamed of since childhood.

Years of infertility ensued, and during that time a lot of emotional turmoil and confusion. I took this setback personally once again and took it as rejection from God. I felt that God had created me to be a mother, and the desire was so overwhelming that I was confused about why God would take it away from me. At the same time, I was praying and believing that God would do a miracle and give us children. I had heard many testimonies of people in the same situation and knew that God was able. But time went on, and no miracle came.

A huge breakthrough came when an Evangelist came and gave me a word of knowledge. He revealed that there were wounds from my childhood that I held deep inside, and that God wanted to heal me from them. God began to show me that some wounds from childhood were so painful to me that I had hidden them so far down that I didn't even recognize that they were there.

Layer by layer, God started bringing things to the surface and healing them. The experience was, at times, very painful, but each time God showed me something and healed me, I felt such joy and liberty in my spirit. It's so strange to know I was so enslaved, and yet I didn't even know it. Only once you are free do you really see what bondage you were under.

In the end, I didn't get the physical miracle I was hoping for. Instead, I got a spiritual one. But with spiritual healing came the confidence to make decisions without fear of displeasing God or stepping out of his will. My husband and I decided to undergo fertility treatment, which had always been an option for us, but I was so bound by fear and insecurity that I resisted making that decision for years. In many ways, I needed spiritual healing before I could take possession of the promise in its fullness. I believe it was God's timing and grace for me to be healed before stepping into motherhood.

In March 2021, six years after losing our first baby, we welcomed our daughter Hallie into the world. Words cannot describe my gratitude towards my heavenly Father for the grace he has shown me. Had I gotten my desires and my own way, I have no doubt in my mind that motherhood would have been filled with such torment and anxiety and not the joy that my heart desired. Now I understand more than ever God's goodness and love towards me, and it's overwhelming for my little human heart to comprehend at times.

REECE, AND MARIAH COOKE WITH BABY HALLIE

It's incredible that God works the way He does in our lives and uses our brokenness to show His goodness. Although before watching this series, I had received deliverance from rejection, God continued His healing work, taking it to a deeper level and showing me incorrect mindsets and thinking patterns that I still needed to deal with. The way you expounded on the issue helped me connect the dots and see even greater revelation in this area than God had previously revealed to me.

I also know first-hand how much this issue can really derail your destiny, hinder your relationship with God and headship, and restrict your Christian walk. With that in mind, I wanted to reach out and extend my thanks to you for teaching on this topic in such depth, as I know it will bring deliverance to many others like me.

God bless, Mariah Cooke

Greg Mitchell
Chapter 16 – Healing from rejection part 2

Prayer: We've now come to the end of the book and I want to pray one final prayer - and that is that God is going to open your eyes and show you His love.

God, as they have read or listened to this book, they now need a miracle and the miracle they need, Lord God, is deliverance that comes through truth. You said the truth will make us free. God, open their eyes. I'm asking as they pray, as they read your word - show them how much You love them. Open the eyes of their understanding so they can know this. God, they already are loved, and when they understand that, let it drive out fear. Perfect love casts out fear. God, show them Your perfect love. Bring a deliverance. Oh, God, as they see that now, correct words; Let them be spoken. Let healing flow in every area of their lives. God, a miracle! Supernatural deliverance comes from the truth. Show them the truth. From this moment, things are going to change in their lives. God, I thank You for the healing that You promise, and I thank You for the revelation You're going to give. In Jesus' name. Amen.

Chris Thorne	Leebon Britoe	Leebon Britoe
Set Free From Rejection	Who am I & Trust issues	I will never leave you
Leebon Britoe	Leebon Britoe	Leebon Britoe
I felt something lift off me	He called me son	I dealt with my anger

Closing Remarks

I want to thank every one of you that you have read, or you have listened to this book. I want to encourage you that you now begin to apply some of the things that God has revealed to you. You lay hold of God's word for yourself. You pray over some of these issues in yourself. Identify areas where you have approached things incorrectly, and repent. Ask God to help you to change. I'm encouraging you; some people have sent me testimonies saying how they went back over the original uprooting rejection series and God began to slowly remove and uproot those roots of rejection, but they have found deliverance. I believe every one of you, that you're going to find Deliverance. You're going to find healing and it's going to flow out in your relationship with God and in your relationships with people, your family, your children, every area of your life. I am believing that God will truly uproot rejection. God bless you.

Recommended Reading

Exposing the Rejection Mindset

     Mark DeJesus   Turning Hearts Ministries

The Power of a New Identity

     Dan Sneed   Sovereign World Publishers

Free Yourself, Be Yourself

     Alan D. Wright   Multnomah Books

Rejection Exposed

     Anthony Hulsebus

The Blessing

     John Trent, Gary Smalley & Kari Trent Stageberg   W Publishing Group

References

Chapter 1

Pastor Rick Renner tells of a time when he was sick for a long time in Junior High School...

https://renner.org/article/if-youre-feeling-unwanted-abandoned-or-rejected-its-time-to-rejoice/

Active Rejection/Passive Rejection
Page 22 Rejection Exposed: Understanding the Root and Fruit of Rejection
Anthony Helsebus

The Impossible Climb: Alex Honnold, El Capitan, and the Climbing Life by
Mark Synnott
Kindle location 512

Chapter 2

Rabbi Shmuley Boteach was friends with Michael Jackson...
CNN June 30, 2009 Jackson rabbi-friend: Singer was 'a tortured, tortured soul'
https://www.cnn.com/2009/SHOWBIZ/Music/06/30/jackson.rabbi/
index.html

Writer/Director Karen Moncrieff speaks about the effect her parent's divorce
USA Today June 10, 2003 Hammering it home: Daughters need dads
https://canadiancrc.com/Newspaper_Articles/
USA_Today_Daughters_Need_fathers_10JUN03.aspx

Chapter 3

A reporter interviewed Marilyn Monroe... Page 72
The Blessing: Giving the Gift of Unconditional Love and Acceptance
John Trent, Gary Smalley, and Kari Trent Stageberg

Chapter 4

Please say you love me... Page 22
The Blessing: Giving the Gift of Unconditional Love and Acceptance
John Trent, Gary Smalley, and Kari Trent Stageberg

Chapter 5
Brené Brown: Shame is...
https://brenebrown.com/articles/2013/01/15/shame-v-guilt/

Tennis pro Andre Agassi was successful...
Agassi reveals more in autobiography
ESPN October 28, 2009

Chapter 6
Jimmy Evans tells a story about a man...
Video: You're Hurting Your Marriage
Ronald Reagan tear down this wall...
Wikipedia: Tear down this wall!

Chapter 7
Social psychologists Carol Tavris and Elliot Aronson...
Mistake were made (but not by me) Page 227

Pastor Fred Craddock/Ben Hooper... Kindle location 2232
Craddock Stories by Fred Craddock   Chalice Press

Chapter 8
Edward Welch said, "What is the result of...people-idolatry?...
When People are Big and God is Small, P&R Publishing, 1997

Chapter 10
In 2013, A 76-year-old Canadian man had to be rescued by firefighters
Hoarder Pinned under Piles of Debris for days
https://www.christianpost.com/trends/hoarder-pinned-under-piles-of-debris-for-days-rescued-with-chainsaw.html

Naomi Judd says, *"Your body hears everything your mind says."*
https://www.brainyquote.com/quotes/naomi_judd_170356

Chapter 16
In 2016, a high school teacher in Colorado named Brittni Darras...
Today.com Teacher writes notes to 130 students after teen's attempted suicide
June 9, 2016

https://www.today.com/news/teacher-writes-notes-130-students-after-teens-attempted-suicide-t97386

S.J. Hill Enjoying God quote:
S.J. Hill Enjoying God: Experiencing Intimacy with the Heavenly Father (Relevant Books 2001)

Who God says I Am: Kindle Location 3371 2nd Edition . Kindle Edition. Exposing the Rejection Mindset Experience Love | Know Who You Are | Empower Your Relationships By Mark DeJesus Turning Hearts Ministries & Transformed You

Acknowledgements

I want to thank all those who encouraged me to turn the "Uprooting Rejection" teaching series into a book.

Many thanks to Daryl Elliot. He encouraged me to write the book, he proofread each chapter, and added valuable suggestions. You are VERY helpful to me.

Once again, many thanks to Steven Ciaccio for your technical help in so many ways. Artwork, video recording, video editing, photo corrections, QR Code insertions, audio recording, and editing. If I had known earlier how smart you are, I would have let you marry my daughter sooner! All that, plus a fine man of God as well. You are an incredible blessing to my life and the Prescott Church.

Thanks to Jesse Morales and Matt Sanderlin for their collective effort in proofreading and catching typos. Matt's additional help in transcribing videos and recording the audio of the Spanish translation is greatly appreciated.

Thanks again to Manuel Delgado, my hard-working Spanish translator. As always, you are using your gifts to bless the Spanish-speaking world. Thanks for proofreading and catching mistakes and typos as you translated the book.

Thanks to the men in other nations that help review the Spanish translation for Manuel. These experienced pastors are university graduates and pastor in different Spanish speaking nations. They draw from their experience in the language and help keep the "Spanish" neutral and readable to all Spanish speaking nations.

Fabian Godano – Argentina.   Heriberto Lapizco – España.
Eladio Junior Ruiz – Peru.

Thanks to Devon Ryals for transcribing the prayers from the videos and helping with filming, video editing and recording.

Thanks to Chris Thorne and Leebon Britoe for their willingness to share on video their stories of uprooting rejection. Your testimonies are not just stories, but powerful tools that God will use to help many other people.

Thanks to Jonathan Heimberg, Jordan Martin and Jayden Martin for recording the testimonies for me.

Thanks to all those who shared their testimonies with me in writing.

Above all, I give thanks to God. Not only did You save me, but You have allowed me to preach Your glorious Gospel. You have helped me so I can help others. You have blessed Lisa and me so much so we can be a blessing. I am still in awe of Your goodness. All around the world, I declare to people, "My Heavenly Father loves me very much!" I do this so they can gain a revelation of Your love for them. May this book be used for Your glory.

About the Author

Greg Mitchell was saved in Prescott, Arizona as a teenager. He met and married his wife Lisa in Perth, West Australia. He was discipled, trained for Pastoral ministry, and sent out of The Potter's House in Perth to pioneer their first church in Launceston, Tasmania, Australia. He Pastored in Melbourne, Victoria, Australia, on three different occasions (2 different churches - Footscray and Dandenong). Greg and Lisa responded to the call of God as missionaries to Johannesburg, South Africa, where God helped them to establish a thriving congregation in the suburb of Eldorado Park. Greg is now Senior Pastor of The Potter's House in Prescott, Arizona. He is the Leader of Christian Fellowship Ministries, International, a church-planting movement with over 3600 churches worldwide (The Potter's House, The Door, Victory Chapel). CFM has churches in 143 nations. Since 1986, Greg has preached the revelation of God's love and His power to heal and deliver: Body, Soul and Spirit. He is also the author of the book Healing Power.

Media Links

To see all photos and videos, follow the link below.

https://www.prescottpottershouse.com/uprooting-rejection-media